"Edstudioz Edtertainment - Remember Me"

Poems, Lyrics, Letters & Messages

Penny N. Pettigrew on behalf of Edwin Henry Kuria

Title: Edstudioz Edtertainment – Remember Me
Subtitle: Poems, Lyrics, Letters & Messages
Author: Penny N. Pettigrew
Genre: Art, Poetry
Reviewed by: Rae C. Bernard

Pacific Book Review Star
Awarded to Books of Excellent Merit

Pacific Book Review

Words are such a powerful tool used to communicate our thoughts, feelings, emotions, and offer encouragement or things of the opposite side of the spectrum. To develop a level of understanding when reading any form of song, especially poetry, takes time and one day it will provide clarity. It can become a beautiful experience. In Edstudioz Edtertainment - Remember Me: Poems, Lyrics, Letters & Messages author Penny N. Pettigrew shares the many well-crafted song lyrics and poetry by a young African man by the name of Edwin Henry Kuria. We're invited into his life and inner thoughts as showcased in this book, which allows us to get an understanding of what it is like being in young Edwin's shoes.

Each poem sets its own tone and emotion; this then invokes the required emotion from its readers, enabling a connection between his work and his readers. Some discussed things about life, while others talked about death, including others that were more in between. As a reader, you'll develop a connection with Edwin based on compassion, strength, love, and support, wanting nothing more than to express that you can relate somehow to him. The emotional journey he's taken can only provide you with a piece of him as lessons learned.

Majority of his song lyrics and poetry were well descriptive about life in Africa, what he's seeing through his eyes, the pain, the struggle, the sorrow of the people of his community. He only wanted to witness his country flourish and shine just like the rest, why was that such a challenge? I understood what he meant completely about dreaming, "of this dark land filled with light and happiness," because a majority of us wants our world to be full of positivity. This resonated with me, people all around the world are going hungry, no shelter, or other bare minimums for survival, and he wanted the evolution for hope and change to occur. Now that I look at it, his visions and dreams slowly began to come true, unfortunately, he won't be able to witness his inner thoughts manifest into reality.

Out of all the song lyrics and poems, the one that stood out to me the most was the one written by his mother. That truly touched me as I sensed the level of pain she experienced through her words. It sent shivers up and down my spine while reading the mother's words as she expresses the loss of her son, hoping that it was a nightmare she may wake up from. He was too young, going based on his written work; I believe he would be amongst the cultural music spins airing on the radio and social media today. The amount of talent this young man possessed indeed has similarities to Tupac Shakur. Unfortunately, no one would ever know how far he would've reached in his life of endless opportunities and potential fame.

I personally, am a huge fan of all forms of creative art, including those with the gift of being a wordsmith. By using our words, we're able to communicate whatever we want, share a time in our lives with others in hopes others will appreciate our truth. That's why, with this book, we are learning about a young man's life growing up in Africa, feeling and understanding where he is coming from. I truly felt his words lifting up from the page, speaking to me and that is the connection I made with Edwin. It was terribly sad to learn of his early demise, even though some of his poetry pointed things out to his readers. almost as if he had a vision of his future. I highly recommend this book to anyone, especially those who were fans and supporters of Tupac's work, something you can relate to.

Published in the United States of America

ISBN 978-1-958518-03-8 (SC)
ISBN 978-1-959173-39-7 (HC)
ISBN 978-1-958518-82-3 (Ebook)

PenBen Publishing
222 West 6th Street
Suite 400, San Pedro, CA, 90731
www.stellarliterary.com

Order Information and Rights Permission:

Quantity sales. Special discounts might be available on quantity purchases by corporations, associations, and others. For details, contact the publisher at the address above.

For Book Rights Adaptation and other Rights Permission. Call us at toll-free 1-888-945-8513 or send us an email at admin@stellarliterary.com.

CONTENTS

R A P

MESSAGES FROM GOD

LAMENTATIONS

LETTERS TO GOD

DEDICATIONS TO MY MOM

THE WILL

PREMONITIONS

REMEMBER ME

FAMILY STORM

LIFT ME UP

IS THERE HOPE?

I MISS YOU

DEDICATIONS

FOREWORD

Edwin Henry Kuria is a child prodigy of sorts; who was inspired to dig deep into his soul to share with his readers and friends' incredible insights about life and its challenges. As a youngster, he wove together his thoughts in writing with rhyme and poise. His way of thinking can easily be associated with the talented and well-educated. The contents of this book therefore defy classification within the context of African writing and poetry, or with regard to the maturity of content. The subject and author in his writing is so profound and mature. In African traditional surroundings, it can be presumed that he must have been stolen by the gods and spent some time away from home, while undergoing divine instruction.

Edwin's keen awareness of events and ideas that he explored in the artistic genre of contemporary African American hip-hop, tells us that art, like music, has no geographical or linguistic boundaries. It communicates and connects us to the same basic human realities of a deeply spiritual nature. There is no doubt that his muses or inspiration was a logical outcome of his specific upbringing in Kenya, and his rather close association with God. Consider also his adoration and longing at the age of 14 and 16, when he attended summer camps in the United States and became acquainted with Pastor Dean Barley, the Founder and President of the Vineyard Camp. He loved every moment of the camp experience. To him, this was a holy haven, which allowed him to honor God in an unsurpassed manner.

Judging from his frequent musical promptings in religious music, and his peculiar conversations with God, I would surmise that his relationship with God and his heightened awareness of God comes close to the solitary mystical experience and probing, that compares with the psalmist in the Bible. The relationship was a fondness that gave him comfort. When he wondered about his future career of becoming a music producer and song writer, he questioned God to give him some kind of direction, while acknowledging his imperfections. Like Jacob, who wrestled with God at

Bethel, Edwin Kuria questioned God, he was convinced that at some crucial points in one's life it was necessary.

There is no dispute about guarding and preserving the legacy, talent and gift of this young man, who lived a very short life, and died under circumstances that were unclear. In African traditional circles, gifted children are endowed with special gifts that must be guarded and preserved. The heart of this gift apparently came from a depth of his being where he always lamented his life without his father, meaning that he was always searching and compensation for his father's absence with the comforting and consoling presence of divine comfort, embodied in the music he produced in his "Edstudioz Edtertainment."

Edwin was a blessing to young people, friends his age and even those older than him, his close relatives and especially his mother. He certainly has been a blessing to me, even though I never knew him until I read his writings. I am certain that he will be a blessing to you too. Although his untimely death continues to perplexc those he left behind, his memory and life is celebrated in this rich and rewarding book.

May Edwin Henry Kuria's spirit continue to live on!

Victor Wan-Tatah,
Author of Religion and Politics in Presedential Elections: The Toxic Influence of Religion in Recent Presidential Elections.
A professor of Philosophy and Religious Studies & Director, Africana Studies Program at Youngstown State University.
Board chair of the Ohio North East Health System.

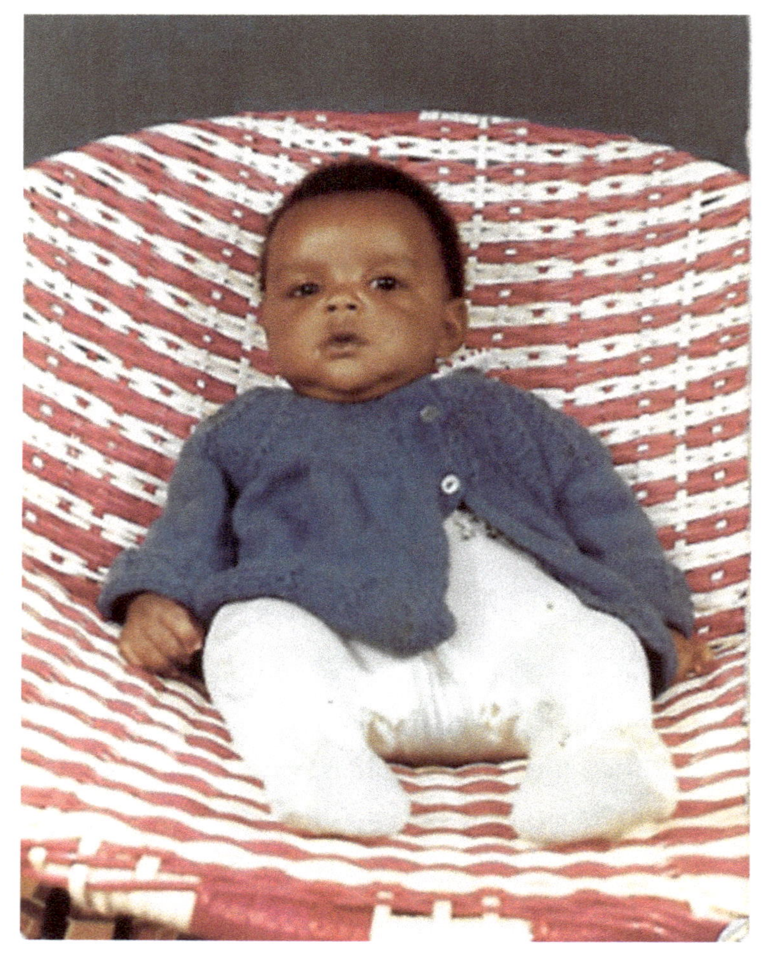

INTRODUCTION

EDWIN HENRY KURIA popularly known as Eddie, was born at a Nairobi Hospital on September 19, 1984 and was raised in Nairobi, Kenya. He was an only child and was raised by his single parent mom Ms Penny N. Kuria. Eddie's mother is now married and goes by her legally married name Penny N. Pettigrew. Eddie came from a family that had musical background and his grandfather the late Mr. Henry Kuria, was at one time the chairman of the Kenya Music Festival. His grandmother Mrs. Ruth Mwihaki Kuria, who trained as a special education teacher in Edinburgh, London was also a great musician. At a very young age, Eddie enjoyed the arts and liked to draw and sing. He also thoroughly enjoyed teaching his mom how to sing the songs he learned at Hospital Hill in Nairobi, where he attended primary school. One of the songs that his mom fondly remembers is *Thy Word Is a Lamp unto My Feet* based on the book of Psalms 119:105. Eddie had learned this song from one of his music teachers in school at the tender age of seven, and every day when he came home, he would attempt to teach it in two-part harmony to his mom. He appeared to be following his grandfather's footsteps. He would teach her the soprano part while he sang the bass part, although his voice had barely broken to carry a deep bass voice. The words of this song are very powerful and one wonders whether Eddie understood the source of inspiration that he was bestowing upon his mom by teaching her the song.

Eddie was an active student and participated in other extracurricular activities, which included soccer, swimming, and several music festival events. Leona Wambui Dondi a former classmate at Hospital Hill School and a dear friend to Eddie writes "Edwin and I met when I was 7. We were in class 3 and were practicing for a live TV variety show in which he would be singing and I would be playing the piano. I can still hear him singing with his sweet voice "Early One Morning…". I didn't know then that 5 years later, he would become one of the greatest people I would ever meet or love. Edwin loved generously and cared deeply for everyone around him. He had big dreams to share his life through music and longed for the day when he would fulfill them. While the world may never get to experience his kind heart or talent, his memory continues to live through us, who were so blessed to be touched by him. I miss him immensely and I'm very fortunate to have shared his wonderful gift of true friendship and love." Leona now lives in Seattle Washington and holds a Master of Science degree in psychology.

As Eddie grew older, he shied away from the singing scene and started taking a keen interest in playing the keyboard. Eddie loved his little keyboard and carried it with him whenever he visited family. He enjoyed entertaining others and demonstrated his God given gift and talent of playing the keyboard without any music lessons. He played well by ear. Although music was part of the school curriculum at Hospital Hill, Eddie's mom paid for private piano lessons so that Eddie could learn how to not only read music but also play written music. Eddie did not appear to like the idea of taking piano lessons, so after a while, his mom decided to allow him do what he liked best, and that was play music by ear.

Following primary school, Eddie was promised by his mom that if he performed well in his Kenya Certificate of Primary Education (KCPE) exams, she would buy him a bigger keyboard. Eddie studied hard and would wake up as early as 4:30 a.m. to study for these exams. Students in Kenya have to be in school by 8:00 a.m. so for one to be up by 4:30 a.m. is a sign of great determination. Although Eddie was an average student, the little effort he put in by waking up early to study, actually paid off. The keyboard was another motivator. It worked. He passed his exams, and the rest is history.

According to Shali Mwadime, a very close and fond friend to Eddie all she has are memories, memories, memories…Shali writes "truly it's never easy to lose a loved one; it's even harder to carry on with life without them. It's taken me ages to do this, but at times you just have to do what you got to do because life never waits for any man to be ready for the challenges that it throws your way." Among the lessons learned from Eddie, Shali quotes some of Eddie's writings which read in part:

> *"Respect is earned but at times we need to disrespect in order to earn respect. In order for you to make it in life, you should always have a dream, a vision of where you want to be, whom you want to become, and what you want to do."*

Shali continues to state that "these were lessons taught by Edwin among many others. Determined to achieve his dreams, he worked hard and loved the Arts. He treasured and adored his keyboard and took his artistic work very seriously. When it came to music, Edwin and his keyboard were inseparable, they were one. Edwin would forever search for open doors to help him reach his goals. He was a go getter, a very persistent gentleman and a true friend. Although he left us at a young age, Edwin in one way or the other, truly achieved his dreams. He is dearly missed to this date." One of Shali's favorite poems written by Eddie includes "No Tearz For Me" a copy of the edited version has been included in this book.

Eddie joined St. Mary's School in Westland Nairobi, a private boys' primary and secondary day school commonly known as Saints. He proceeded to year eight of the General Certificate Examination (GCE) program. This program is a popular academic program with parents who want their children to get varied curricula that would prepare them to continue their studies overseas. According to the school web site this program "also develops students' skills in creative thinking, enquiry and problem solving, and gives them excellent preparation for their senior high school years and university education" (St. Mary's School, 2014).

The 4th president of Kenya, Uhuru Kenyatta, also attended this school in 1979. Girls along with boys are admitted to the International Baccalaureate (IB) diploma course. Lupita Nyong'o, the first Kenyan Oscar award winner of the *Academy Award for Best Supporting Actress*, attended the IB program in the same school. She had a stunning performance as Cinderella where she acted with her co-star Gatumia Waithaka in the Cinderella play. Eddie was also a part of the annual school plays during the time when Lupita was an IB student in St. Mary's School. Just like in primary school, Eddie was an active student and participated in other extracurricular activities, which included music, drama and swimming (where he won several swimming championship awards). Today, Eddie would be proud to realize how fortunate he was to have attended school with some famous people.

Above: The fourth president of Kenya President Uhuru Kenyatta

Below: Edwin performing with other Saints students during a school musical

At the Vineyard Camp in Westfield, North Carolina

At the Vineyard Camp in Westfield, North Carolina

Although the main reason of Eddie's mom to have Eddie join St. Mary's School was to have him join the school orchestra, this idea did not go as planned. The instructors required that a student have the ability to read music. Eddie still wanted to play music by ear. He had his own way of thinking. This to him, this was a God given talent that did not require the ability to have to read music and he wanted to utilize it in a free spirited way. Although Eddie was taking music as one of the subjects in the class, he decided to drop the music class when the time came for students to drop the classes they did not want to pursue. He decided to take art.

Eddie's mom is the only person who truly supported and gave him the chance to use his God given talent as he had desired. One of his teachers from St. Mary's School Ms Evelyn Mung'au sent an email to his mom and this is what it read in part: "Anyone who knows me will tell you that I am a noisy extrovert and that is how I met Edwin. I was in my element – 100 words per minute, barely letting Edwin answer any of my questions but at the same time finding out that he was exactly the kind of person that I hoped came out of St. Mary's: A young man unabashed of his unorthodox career plans and looking forward to creating his own niche in the world. In his straightforward and open ways Edwin showed his teachers and friends even not-so-close staff like myself what a great job you did as a mom." She continues to write stating "...you can take comfort in the knowledge that through Edwin you made the world a better place for letting us see what it means to let those you love live their dreams and feel no shame that it is not what everybody else felt was important..."

Eddie was a staunch Christian and he always excelled in his Christian religious education (CRE) classes. His teacher at St. Mary's School Sister Candida, was always amazed at how well Eddie knew the bible. From a young age, Eddie attended Sunday school faithfully at the Nairobi Pentecostal Church, Valley Road. His mom always bought him the Christian comic books which were sold outside the church after most services. These comic books helped Eddie understand the bible as they were simple and gave clear depictions of what transpired in both the Old and New Testament.

During his teenage years while watching one of the preachers on television, Eddie gave his life to Christ, and was born again. He attended summer camp at the Vineyard Camp in Westfield, NC at the age of 14 and 16 where he left his own niche. The children and staff loved him. Eddie enjoyed the positive experience of the spiritual focus of the camp. He loved every moment of the praise and worship that took place in Dean Barley's home (the Founder/President of The Vineyard Camp). On his return from the camp he would talk about how he would one day have a home just like Pastor Dean's. To him this was a holy haven, and the camp experience immensely allowed Eddie to honor God in an unsurpassed manner. He strongly believed in God, and as you will read from his writings, he had a very close relationship with God. As we all know or have been told by our forefathers, you never question God. There were times when Eddie would get so frustrated by all the negativity about his interest and attempts of becoming a music producer and song writer, that he had no choice but to question God. He admits that he was not perfect and he begged God to forgive him whenever life turned its claws on him. He always used to say "only God can judge me now."

The writings in this book are just some of the work that the mom managed to salvage. There are many more writings that may have been thrown out in the trash just to keep Eddie's room tidy. His room which he named "Edstudioz" was always full of papers and sometimes the only way out was to throw them away. Eddie also adored artists like Tupac Shakur. His friends would probably argue that the use of the word "adore" is in an understatement. His "Edstudioz" bedroom wall was full of Tupac pictures. He owned every single CD he could lay his hands on that had the name Tupac on it. Reuben Chege, a former classmate and friend at Saints writes "I have a lot of memories from Eddy." He continues to state how he genuinely cared for Edwin as they used to talk about a lot of stuff. Reuben says "I constantly read his poems and gave him encouragement, calling him the next "Tupac" as he was so fond of the rapper back then."

In August 2001 and following graduation in May of the same year at Daystar University, Eddie's mom left for the United States of America to pursue further studies and to prepare a place for Eddie's music career. Eddie was left behind and was residing with his aunt Mrs. Joyce G. Ng'ang'a, uncle (the late Mr. Jackson Kamau Ng'ang'a) and his four cousins Nicholas Kamau, Joan Wanjiru, Cynthia Mwihaki, and Henry Kuria. Eddie was left behind so that he could complete his final year in the GCE program before joining his mom in the states. During a visit to the United States by Prof. Godfrey N. Lule, one of Eddie's mom's closest friend and confidant, she bought Eddie a Tupac T-shirt. Prof. Lule was kind enough to deliver it to Eddie's aunt on his return trip. Eddie was ecstatic on receiving the T-shirt and he treasured it just as much as he treasured his keyboard. Below is a picture of Eddie wearing the said T-shirt during his visit to see his mom in the U.S. in March 2002.

In January 2002, Eddie completed his final exams and with the help and support of Prof Lule, he left Kenya on March 17, 2002 to visit his mom in the United States. While there, he also attended an interview at the Guildford Technical Community College (GTCC) where his mom had applied for him to join the Entertainment Technology Program. Eddie had been offered admission to the college and Todd Dupree, the coordinator of this program who interviewed Eddie, was excited to have a student from Africa. Eddie's visit to GTCC was breath taking and he enjoyed the atmosphere at the music school which was filled with keyboards and other musical instruments. Eddie was in awe! He could now see a light at the end of the tunnel. On setting his eyes in the class where he was about to become one of the entertainment technology students, he turned toward his mom with a big smile and with his eyes wide open and told her "this is the kind of atmosphere that I really like" and you could see the joy all over his young handsome face!

Since Eddie's GCE results and official school grades had not all been submitted from the London office, he was required to take the placement test. He spent most of the days preparing for this test. He even spent hours in the library just to prepare for the test. Every evening while his mom came home from school, they would share stories of his stay with his aunt, uncle and cousins in Kenya but before going to bed, he made sure he studied some more. The date for taking the placement test was drawing near and Eddie appeared ready.

On April 3rd, 2002 Eddie's mom woke up early to attend class at the University of North Carolina Greensboro (UNCG) where she was a psychology student. She was scheduled to take a statistics exam in the afternoon. She left home early and did not have time to prepare any breakfast for Eddie. According to the African tradition, men do not perform house chores such as cooking, but Eddie had agreed to defy this rule. He was going to not only prepare his own breakfast but also prepare dinner for his mom. Eddie's mom was so excited that she was going to come home and find dinner prepared by Eddie. The first thing she did when she got hold of a computer was to send an email to her sister Nancy in Kenya informing her that she was going to eat a meal prepared by Eddie. During break, Eddie's mom went to see her mathematics and statistics lecturer Ms Walker G. Weigel and spent some time revising. At 12 noon she was to meet with other classmates to do some additional revision prior to the statistics test at 2:00 p.m. As she waited to meet the other students, she had this strong instinct that kept on telling her to go home. After waiting for her friends for a period of 10 minutes with no sign of them coming, she decided to follow her instinct and left.

On arrival at her apartment, she found police cars and several people standing outside. She had no idea that all these people were actually at her apartment. On arrival at the door, she was surprised to see her door wide open as she walked towards it. One of the police officers Detective LeJeune asked her which house she was going to and she pointed toward the door where everyone was standing. The police officer asked her if she knew the young man who was residing there and how she was related to him. She answered in the affirmative explaining that that was her son. The first thought that came to her mind was that perhaps Eddie had burned the house while cooking. Remember, African men do not typically cook. She asked them what was going on. She dropped her book bag and walked her way through the crowd and into the apartment. As she walked in toward the bathroom, she saw blood on the carpet and asked what was going on. One of the other police officers a detective Lee Walker, gently held her by the hand and sat her down to break the sad news. He told her that when the paramedics arrived at the scene that her son did not have a heartbeat. She was uncontrollable and did not want to hear those words. It was alleged at the time that Eddie had chocked on an orange he was eating.

The maintenance employee who worked for Pickering and Company at the time, had come to check if the fire extinguishers were working, and was the one who called 911 after he found Eddie lying face down on the floor. One wonders whether Eddie got scared after hearing the knock on the door by a stranger or worse still, the opening of the door with a key by the maintenance guy. Having arrived in the country barely two weeks, Eddie did not know what the maintenance procedures were and that the maintenance people had the ability to open the door and enter the apartment when performing maintenance checks. The mom had not prepared him for this. Although he was aware that the maintenance guy was scheduled to come on that day, the loud knock on the door may have scared him to death. He may have attempted to run to the bathroom for cover when he heard the maintenance guy opening the door with a key. He probably was eating his orange at the time and perhaps tripped and fell. These are all speculations and will remain so until we meet again. When questioned, the maintenance guy said Eddie was breathing at the time he made the call. The reason why the maintenance guy was doing a follow up on the fire extinguishers was due to a fire at the time at some apartments on Spring Garden Road in Greensboro, NC where an upset girlfriend had set a fire to her boyfriend's couch which led to four deaths and total destruction of the apartments.

With the monitory support provided for by many Kenyans in the United States and Kenya (both known and unknown to Eddie's mom), Eddie's remains were transported back to Kenya on April 10, 2002. He was laid to rest on April 13, 2002. Eddie's mom chose to celebrate Eddie's life during the funeral which was held at the Nairobi Pentecostal Church, Valley Road. He was buried at his grandparents' home in Waguthu, Kiambaa location, in Kiambu district next to his great grandfather, great grandmother, aunt and now his grandfather and grandmother.

The cruel hand of death took Eddie's life just when his dreams were starting to become a reality. Why would one not then question God? He was an only child, high spirited, friendly, and a healthy boy at that. He was so focused and determined in achieving his goals no matter what people said. The autopsy results that took three and a half months indicated that he died a natural death of undetermined cause. His death remains a mystery and it is difficult to have closure without having a definite cause of death.

The writings in this book are therefore Eddie's own writings. The spelling of some the words have not been altered so as to maintain the originality of Eddie's writings. He has several writings lamenting about his life as a child without the presence of an earthly father, and makes several premonitions about his death. He also laments about several other issues including the fact that people failed to acknowledge his God given talent. Is this an issue that society has failed to acknowledge for the sake of requiring our children to become book smart? You be the judge.

It has been many years now since Eddie passed on to higher glory. He probably has produced a couple of records wherever he is at his "Edstudioz Edtertainment". For his mom, life will never be the same without him. The lack of a clear indication as to why the cruel hand of death had to snatch away her only son will always remain a mystery. She has no closure, but she has to move on with life as the clock does not stop ticking. It is honorable that she has taken the time to have Eddie's writings published. It is time for Eddie's writings to stop wasting away in the shelves, and for the world to read and be inspired by the lamentations and premonitions of this young African teenage prodigy. As you read through these poems, lyrics, and writings, do not rush in being judgmental. Try to find the symbolical meaning that this young teenager was trying to communicate, and remember his words "only God can judge me now".

IN THE EVENT OF MY DEMISE

When my heart can beat no more
I hope I die for a principle or a belief
that I have lived for
I will die before my time because I
already feel the shadow's depth
So much I wanted to accomplish before
I reached my death
I have come to grips with the possibility
and wiped the last tear from my eyes
I loved all who were positive in the
Event of my demise

_2Pac, 1992
Re-written by E.K.
2002

ORIGINALLY WRITTEN AND INSPIRED BY THA LATE TUPAC SHAKUR

Pliz wake me when I am free,
I cannot beat captivity.
Where my culture I am told,
Of no significance,
I whithered & died,
In Ignorance.
But my Inner eyez see,
A race, who reigned as King,
In antoher place.
The green trees were rich & full,
And every man spoke of beautiful men & women,
Together as equal.
War was gone,
Because all was at Peace.
But now, like a nightmare,
I woke to see, that I live,
Like a prisoner of poverty;
Pliz, wake me when I am free.
I cannot bear captivity,
For I would rather be stricken blind,
Than to live without,
Expression of mind.

GOD

When I woz alone & had nothing,
I aksed for a friend to help me bear tha' pain.
No one came, except God.
When I needed a breath to rize from my sleep,
No one could help me, except God.
And all I saw woz sadness,
And I needed answerz;
No one heard me, except God.
So when am asked, who I'd give my unconditional love to,
Look for no other name, except God.

IN MY MUSIC

I have loved music, almost all my life. I feel as though it's part of me; that which makes me feel right. It's a blessing from the LORD GOD ALMIGHTY, that I have been granted the talent of music. I hope to produce, not that which comes from other peoples thoughts, but that which I feel in my heart.

To all who may witness my rising, I hope to shine or rather produce that which shall give joy and happiness to all. I believe the LORD has granted me the skill and the ability to do what's best; my heart is able to express. It has never been easy to be the best, and though I may never be, I believe that GOD shall open the gates for me, to which I hope to follow in the works of my life and career i.e. music.

Those I may hurt, I beg the LORD to forgive me, and you too, to forgive me. There'z nobody so perfect in the world, except my LORD JESUS CHRIST who lived without sin. Therefore, I believe I am not perfect, so I accept all my mistakes and hurting that I may cause. I hope to love all, for hate is like a drop of ink in pure water. And so as I love, I hope not to hate, for this shall spread and consume my heart, and darken the light in me, which once shone so bright. I am praying that GOD shall help me overcome these things that may lead me to worse sinning.

With GOD, all things are possible. My hopes seem to be slowly shattered, by the belief of many who tell me music in this country (meaning - Kenya) can never be a career in which you hope to succeed.

To my LORD, I believe in my visionz, you have seen my hopes and dreamz. With these I hope you shall show me a way in which you will lead and I will follow. I believe I will succeed in my missions and journeyz with your help. I have loved you and always will.

CASIO

ED STUDIOZ ENTERTAINMENT

To date, this would be the name of an entertainment label in the foundation of a dream. It would be a life testimony for Africa az a whole and basic day to day life, here in Africa. This is my dream, and a contribution of my work to Africa. "Ed-Studioz" would not only be an expression from Africa, but would be more like a message, to the rest of the world.

The entertainment label az I would hope, would grow letting the world know, that there is a talent in my pride; the black continent. The warz, the killings, the struggles in Africa, would all be layed on the table and expressed through our music. Based on hip-hop, reggae, R&B and many other verbal ways of communication this label would come to be embraced by the world az Africa consists of different cultures.

Swahili, English, French, and slang (mixture of Swahili and English) would be some of the languages used under "Ed-Studioz". The music we produce, may be enjoyed by people of all ages, for what this label's about to bring, has been heard before, only this time, It's coming from Africa.

I believe we've got talent, and abilities that the outside worlds have underestimated us for. I think too many have talked about Africa, and so I believe, that It's the Africans chance to speak out for themselves, so that we may not be overshadowed by the rest of the world.

"Ed-Studioz ENTERTAINMENT" belongs to Africa, and not only those who may help in the growing of one of the most multi-talented labels the world may ever see. This one, is not for East, West, Central, North or South Africa, this is for the whole of Africa, so that we may be in union as brothers and sisters as we are meant to be. This is my dream and In God'z handz I lay my all.

EDWIN KURIA

ECCLESIASTES: 7:3-9 & 9 17 (FYI: THIS APPEARS TO BE EDWIN'S INTERPRETATION)

- Sorrow is better than laughter; It may sadden your face,
  But It sharpens your understanding
- Someone who is always thinking about happiness is a fool.
  A wise person thinks about death
- It is better to have wise people reprimand you,
  Than foolish people singing you praises
- When a fool laughs, It is like thorns cracking in fire;
  It doesn't mean a thing
- You may be wise, but if you cheat someone,
  You are acting like a fool. If you take a bribe,
  You ruin your character.
- The end of anything is better than its beginning
  Patience is better than Pride
- Keep your temper under control, It's foolish to harbor a grudge
  9:17 It is better to listen to the quiet words of the wise,

  - Than the shouts of a ruler at a council of fools

THERE'Z A DREAM

There'z a dream
And there'z God in it
There'z a stream
And flows eternally.

There'z a vizion,
Unseen, by anyone living
There'z a mission
And I'm hoping to complete it.

In the night,
I wipe a tear drop, before I sleep,
Happy, for I might
Just be that dream.

There'z a dream
And God will fulfil it
And the eternal dream
Flowz within me.

L*OVIN'* **A**lwa'z E**K**uria

UNTITLED

I have a dream
But It's hard to fulfil it
I have dream
And a talent, that I wanna use to the limit.
I have a gift
That many have praised me for
But deep inside of me,
I know all praise, is for the LORD.
There's a record playing in my head
An endless tune,
That keeps playing every day.
An emotion,
Flows with this tune
And when I let it out,
There'z gonna be a message for you.
There'z a rap star,
Making more and more millions.
He's headed far,
He's on a different mission.
I shed a tear
For I know what the future holds for me
And my greatest fear,
Will I ever get to fulfill my dream?

UNTITLED

It's like a dream
Just to be a star
Will I ever make it
Though am filled with hope in my heart
My lyrics like a magic potion
Words full of emotions
My trials and tribulations
And all my pain is shown
Looking at the stone walls
Inside my bedroom
Have Lot's of money and carz
Though I waz never meant to
I want the fame
So I can go a lot of places
When you hear my name
And I see the smile on your faces
They tell me am too young
So don't get your hopes high
Soon az my lyrics are sung
I picture people going wild
I can't lie
Am full of hope
Determination in my songz
Got me going strong
Maybe through the yearz
I will learn my lesson
So many laughs and tearz
In my rap pforession
So let me get paid
Az I struggle to survive
I just wanna make it
Dreamz of an African child

NOT TOO FAR

Hoping to make it through
Another night still the screamz
Fade away in my sleep.
Await to see, the rising of the sun
Fulfilin' all my dreamz
Another day in the motherland.
I can't sleep cauze it's hard
And I don't wanna face it
But I believe in my heart
Someday am gonna make it.
Somebody help me
Wipe all these tearz away
So many worriez
Hoping for an easier way.
Visionz of a paradise unknown to man
Can't comprehend what they mean
Somebody help me understand.
    There'z so much they've got to tell
    They trapped me in a cell
    A grown man's hell

UNTITLED

It came as a surpise
The dreams of an African child
Finally came true to light
And I'll be aiming for great heights
Always hoped
That one day I'd be a star
Even though it was hard
I still believe in my heart
I remember the holidays
With a can of spray
Singing hip hop hurray
Hoping that I would make it
A change
Iz all we needed
The fame
Had got me heated
Make some money
If I've got earn a living

HERE IZ THE WORLD

Here I chill, contemplate on my skill.
Struggling with possibilities, I know my will.
Here the dream starts, Here I speak my heart.
Let the stage curtains draw apart, Here Iz the world.

NB: For every performance on or off stage, I place God first in everything before I say these
Words and If He wishes, let me make It.

L*OVIN'* **A**lwa'z E**K**uria

THE REVELATION OF MY FAME

Each day a child iz born. It's sweetness brings joy to all, and it's memoriez az It growz, are always special, in the hearts of all who knew it. In the birth of my fame, when I finally begin my journey to fulfilin' all my dreamz, I hope to spread joy and love, in the words I use, to express what's in my heart.

I hope to follow the right path, and do according to what I believe. The BEST things come az a result of patience. In my learning of the skill of what It takes to be a star, I hope the lessons shall be fruitful, to the works of my hand. I've learnt to accept my mistakes, and to the LORD I pray, hoping that He may change my wayz.

May my vision and His presence, go hand in hand, for He seez beyond the vizionz of men. When I cry, may the tearz that I shed be of expression of love, for I love all who have been there to help me see a brighter day. If no man iz perfect, then not even I deserve to be considered so. For even in the strugglez of doing right, I know I have caused harm to many. May I be forgiven for the wrong that I've done to these, for at the time, it seemed like the only right thing.

To my mother, I pray that God shall bless her, and grant teaching so that she may live by His will and when she finally parts from this earthly life, she may share the joy, that He brought to me in my many dreamz in my youth. I love you Mama, even though you doubted my dreams, I hope I will fulfil all of them, and God willing, in their blessingz I hope to make some of your dreams come true.

I toast a glass of wine, to all my peerz and other friendz who may have passed away, and in their demise, may their memoriez consume a special part in my heart.

I get prepared, to finally take my place, for I believe, it's been preserved by someone great. To whoever this may be, I appreciate the fact, that they've opened the gates to which I hope to lead the way.

In the birth of my fame, may I not forget my principles, and be misled by the fruits of fame & fortune. May pride not consume my heart, and may I remember all who were special, to the dawning of this day.

Before the sun has risen, may the celebration be prepared, for I am about to rise to high limits. I thank my LORD, for I feel this is what He'z laid out for me. May my garl love me for who I am, and may she be by my side, always. She is part of me, therefore am not complete without her. Whoever she may be, may she be a gift and a blessing from my LORD.

As before the sun has set, and darkness haz overcome this land, may my fame be laid to rest with love and passion. My body to all, shall be stolen from your sight and never, in your gentle armz, will I be held. Before I die, I hope to cherish each moment that I share with you all. I love u all, and this I write, for it is my revelation, unto my handz.

BE BLESSED

L*OVIN'* E**K**uria

THE (UNFINISHED) CD

Dedicated to the boyz I love

1. Somewhere watchin' me
2. Say a prayer for me
3. Hear your heart speak
4. You're my type of lady
5. Don't let It stop
6. Valley of passion
7. In my last goodbye (lude)
8. How can I explain
9. If only you knew
10. Hopin' to see the sun

BONUS TRACKS

1. I'll brake you off
2. Inside of me

13. Smilin' caskets

(To homeez dead & alive)

Dedicated to the boyz I love

1. Somewhere watchin' me
2. Say a prayer for me
3. Hear your heart speak
4. You're my type of lady
5. Don't let It stop
6. Valley of passion
7. In my last goodbye (lude)
8. How can I explain
9. If only you knew
10. Hopin to see the sun

BONUS TRACKS

11. I'll brake you off
12. Inside of me

13. Smilin' caskets (To homies dead & live)

SOMEWHERE WATCHIN' ME

Each time when I sleep
There'z an angel watchin' me
Guiding all my dreamz
Am protected by the wings
He walks with me
And talks with me
Never leaves me
He's somewhere watchin' me

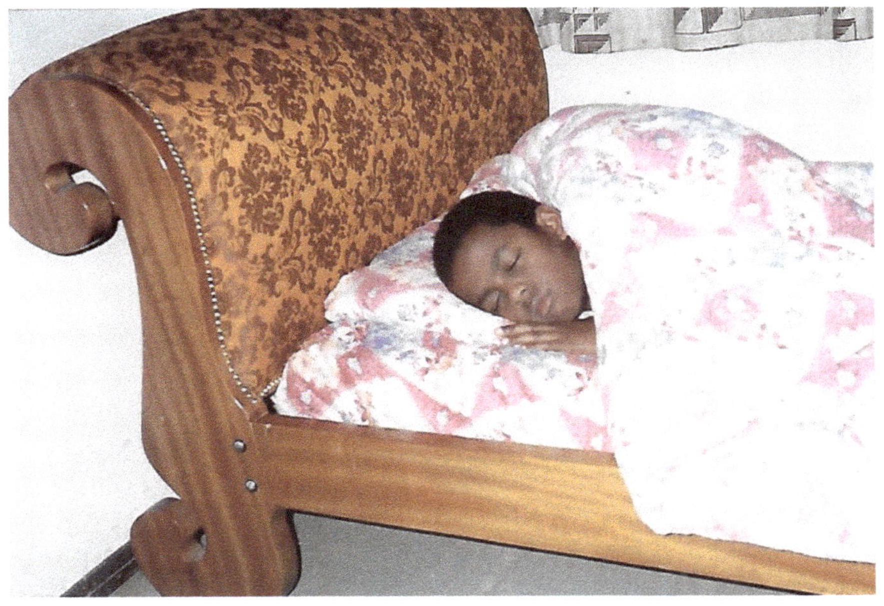

LOVIN' EKuria

SAY A PRAYER FOR ME

Even though you may wrong me
You're still my homie
And when nobody carez for me
I know you'll say a prayer for me

Eyez of scorn, looked upon me, since I waz born
Daddy waz long gone, alone me and mama had to carry on
Filled with talent, searching for a better chance
When am finally a man, maybe someone can understand
Holdin' on, to a bottle of cologne
Helpless dreamer, And I waz rappin' to the mirror
Clutching' a pound, screamin' aloud "WESTI"
Thinkin' about, The day when I finally make It
Trapped in sin, If you know what I mean
I was lost in dreamz, that I waz hopin' to fulfil
Seein' young kidz, Holdin' on to a cell phone
What happened to me? Now grown, still dead broke
Headed home, and az a kid I was lonely
Needed more, So I could fit with my homiez
Hopin' you'll be there for me,
Every day I need you homie,
Take my hand and hold me,
And pliz say a prayer for me

HOW CAN I EXPLAIN

How can I explain?
When am in my sleep
How can I explain
About my endless dream
How can I explain
About the way I feel
How can I explain
What's deep inside of me
How can I explain
That I wanna make It far
It's so hard to say
But someday I'll be a star
How can I explain
Is It cause of the pain
In my search for fame?
How can I explain
About the voice that talks to me
And so I'm prayin' to God
To fulfil my dream
(Someday)
I know I'll make it (Yeah)
(And when am laid) inside my grave
There'll be somebody else to say
What I tried to explain
And If I make It to heaven
(In your heart)
I will know how to explain.

Written by: Ed-studio CEO
and producer and
Artist: Eddy kuria
Performed by: Eddy

IF ONLY YOU KNEW

Forgive me father, cause at this point am feelin' hopeless
Losin' focus, and feelin' helpless
Findin' no meaning from the many lessons
Raized without a father figure
Had to adjust quicker
No brother nor sister
And riches is all that I could picture
Dressed in torn flesh
Eyez of scorn look upon me
Sin became my own
Flowing through my weak bones
A victim
Of not believing in realism
My existence based on the fulfillment
Of all my endless dreamin'
Shattered hopes
But still I had to cope
Memoriez of my fantasiez
The man I always wanted to be
Material eyez
Got me consumed
In this world of liez
Tell the truth
Sometimes I just wish that I could die
Crying cauze of the pain
Strange, whispers of rage
And If I make It
Will the future know just how much It takes
On my kneez and so I pray
Hoping for a brighter day
Before am laid to rest
If only you knew just how much It takes

HOPIN' TO SEE THE SUN

Hopin' to see the sun when my dayz would come
So many goals in my life ever since I was young
My family consists of my mama and me
4 Born with dreamz was the team That I alwa'z roll with
Hold me, somebody say a prayer for me
At fourteen and my family waz my homiez and me
Broke and blind, and money was hard to come by
8 tryin' to kill what we left behind
Tryin' to rhyme with the teli
When BIG and Makaveli
Would be bumpin' loud speakers all over Westi
With a paper and pen, a dream swimmin' in my head
Though It's hard to comprehend
4 I know someday I'll be a legend
Drunk from life, so you can see how I feel inside
Each time am speakin', Iz an expression of my feeling
Fear inside my heart, Az am copin' with the dark
Tearz aside as I brush, Hopin' to see the sun

Though It's hard
I know someday we'll make It
And in my heart
I know someday I'll see the sun

Sky's the limit, and how much cash in a minute
Will all this rhyme spittin', change my way of livin'
Fantasiez of the game, Az I pictured inside
Not knowin' there would be a day, when It would be my life
Industry, will I survive or will It have the best of me
Misery, captured the gifted some layin' in the cemetery
Livin' lavish, Big cribs and fine wheelz
Dreamin' of havin', If I make It to the big screen.

SHALI'LL ALWAYZ (BE INSIDE OF ME)

Though times we may part
You'll always be inside my heart
And with that face
Shali, no one could take your place
Sad tearz fill my eyez
And times I wanna die
Cauze sweet dreamin' and fantasizin'
realizin' you're not mine
Four long years
Since the day that we first met
Dreamin' about the chance
When I finally be your man
Shali your special
An angel sent down from heaven
LORD knows only your smile
Gives me joy inside, and you're nice
I wanna marry, have a family and keep you happy
Till that day
Shali'll (always'z be inside of me x2)

SMILIN' CASKETS

Don't you cry
Don't you cry after am gone
Don't you try to blame my LORD
Don't you cry cause now am home
Don't shed a tear
When am finally out of here
Pass the flame unto my peerz
Unto thoze that I grew with
I had my chance
To express my love for you
But you paid me back in pain
And now n no more again
Rocks of hurting
That you picked
That you threw so hard at me
I just wanted to see you happy
But now It's too late now am buried
So
WILL YOU SHOW ME LOVE
INSIDE MY SMILIN'CASKETS
WILL YOU THROW A ROSE
INSIDE MY SMILIN' CASKETS
CAUSE YOU WILL ALWA'Z BE THE GARL I LOVED
WILL THEY BURY YOU
CLOSE TO MY SMILIN' CASKETS
SO I CAN FEEL YOU WARMTH
INSIDE MY SMILIN' CASKETS
IF I HAD A CHANCE
THEN I WOULD PRAY YOU LAY WITH ME
I NEVER HAD A CHANCE WITH YOU
AND NOW AM MISSIN YOUR SMILE
    (In the smilin' caskets wishin'
    In the smilin' caskets missin'
    In the smilin' caskets wonderin'
    Why you never loved me)

LYRICS

TO MY MAMA

Remember back at that time
when I was a little baby mama
little time always cryin to get
milk. Had lots of dreamz
to be big n though thingz seemed
really tight she always had me
goin, never to quit on ma' fight.
Now I c ma'self # n' thank
God for my mama raized me
with a true heart ain't no
mother like her. Though I caused
you hell. Kept in ma' mind what
you said, given ya'self in work
to ensure my happiness.
You truly awesome in ma' life
brought joy even when I cried. Glad
to be ya' baby boy as a man
ya' luv iz right. Ain't no one else
mean more than what you do to
me on ma' knee's I pray each

day you may live eternally.
Seein' tha' pain I caused n' tears stream down my eyez, Sit back n' wonder why I did theze thingz to you. I woz a fool but still I cared for you want you to feel ma' luv cuz thiz goez out for you

Chorus: N' to my mama wordz can't express how I feel thingz you did for me am grateful for all you did Rizin' from bed in da' mornin' with ya' sight then sing no worriez thank you for raizin' me n' I luv you mommy

While still a kid never knew about my father when timez got real rough always depended on my mama. Some people laughed

TO MY MAMA

Remember back at tha' time when I was a little baby mamaz little diem, always cryin' to get milk. Had lots of dreamz to be big n though thingz seemed real tight she alwa'z had me goin', never to quit on ma' fight.

Now I c ma'self n' thank God for my mama raized me with a true heart ain't no mother like her. Though I caused you hell kept in ma' mind what you said, given ya'self in work to ensure my happiness.

You truly awesome in ma' life brought joy even when I creid. Glad to be ya baby boy az a man ya luv is right. Ain't no one else means more than what you do to me on ma kneez I pray each day you may live eternerly.

Seein' tha' pain I caused n' tearz stream down my eyez. Sit back n' wonder why I did these things to you. I woz a fool but still I cared for you want you to feel ma' luv cuz this goes out for you

CHORUS: N' to my mama words can't express how I fell thingz you did for me am grateful for all you did. Rizin' from bed in da' mornin' wich ya' sight they ain't no worries thank you for raizin' me n' I luv you mummy

While still a kid never knew about my father when timez got real rough always depended on my mama. Some people laughed at me when I said I never knew him thought I woz real foolish but hadn't been my wish.

Hold on gotta be strong n' I had to move on in school seein daddy'z kissin' their kidz good bye. On ma' bed I'd lay n' cry sleep as I wonder why but now c havin' a mama'z tha' greatest in life.

Started from nowhere but now we getting' somewhere all alone you been ma' star n' this comez straight from ma' heart want you to feel this your ma' realest n' I mean it

CHORUS

WRITING OF A DAY 2 COME

My opinion for tomorrow
Iz an argument of today
Yet It waz an Idea yesterday
But a useless expression to the world.

From reflecting on my life
I realized what waz
And from realizing what waz,
I perfected what Iz,

My concentration of thoughts
Developed into dilute Ideas
With flava in my expressionz
Az I bumped out a feeling by song.

Yo! Check It!!
Dangerous are the participants of thought
For each view results to confusion in conscience.
Collectiveness results in unison of view
And calmness plus composure brings out respectable meaning & understanding of opinion

Rhythm entraps the audience
And lyrical flow entangles them into question.
Thus, an expression Iz embraced or disliked
And judgement of fame remainz in the audience handz.

Yesterday passed, and left me in question,
An Idea of my opinion and view for today.
With a difference I took today with caution
In this writing of a day to come.

SOMETIMES I GET LONELY

Got pushed out from the womb, az my mama took the pain
Inside a room screaming loud and finally here I came
Born alone and daddy waz long gone, I never got to see his face
4 It makes me pain knowing He left this trace
Barely seven yearz I can recall all my peerz
How they talked about their daddy'z, wishing mine could be here
I grew alone, me, my mama and a stranger
8 I could not blame her though filled so much anger
Grew into my early teenz, searching for better meanz
Of making profit, while my team were alcoholics
Gaining fame from the words I sang, It hurts knowing,
4 I make friends cauze I had some cash
But now I sit alone and write a song
I realized, I was born to be on my own
I close my eyez, say a prayer az tearz invade my head
8 No more smilez, No one carez, am lost in the dark
And If I could go back
Inside my mama'z womb,
LORD knows I would not waste a minute.
To change back inside
So many I've lost, But I'll make It against all oddz
4 So many I mourn for, But life goes on
Am drowning my pain,
Inhaling desperate hopes, searching for better dayz
Dear Jesus If you hear us or see us
Give us a hope, broke African child,
8 Trying to cope with the fast life
Times I wanna cry, Times I wanna die.
Times when my biggest smile, could not hide, how I feel inside
4 I wanna make It but It's hard cause am dying inside
Sometimes I need a homie, sometimes, need you to hold me
Sometimes I need you to say a prayer for me
And though times It seemz ok, through the night look to the mourning
When you could hold me sometimes I get lonely

FOR HE GIVES LIFE AND TAKES IT AWAY

Sitting here alone, Az I contemplate
Crying Reminiscing on my homie; let's cut to the chase
Am here Father on my kneez, searching for a reazon
Why my friend had to die, Pleaze tell me why
So many separated and went different wayz,
But He and I still remainded the same
And now He's gone, to another place, Oh!!
Father send an angel to heal my pain
And how I wish, You could pliz forgive his sins
The game you put us in, made It hard to live
And If my man get's to heaven (where I know he rests)
I'll still be singing this song, Trying to carry on
BRIDGE And I'm just hoping you might feel me
I'm here in place of my homie
You gave Him life, gave me a brother, now you've taken
And Dear God now am praying

Here I am, A lonely man
Watch over my friend, he's only a man
Won't you forgive us, For not knowing our purpose
But blinded by this life that we live,
Look through my heart, See the scarz of this world
It's hard x 2

UNTITLED

V1

I saw your mama crying
Tearz and wondered how you died
I couldn't believe
It was your last goodbye
So many left worried
Drown in your loving memoriez
Friendz and familiez, and,
Uncontrollable weeping
And now am all alone
God, to help me carry on
It's seemed like a dream
Can't still believe that you're gone
The pain and sorrow
I know a brighter day will follow
And through the rainz storm
I wonder how many more

HOW MANY MORE TO GO
REST IN PEACE WITH THE LORD
IT'S HARD TO GO ON
ALL ALONE NOW THAT YOU'RE GONE
AND EVEN AS WE MOURN
I KNOW IT'S HEAVEN AT HOME

V2

Your gal was screaming
Mama couldn't help but weep
The pain too deep
Seemed like you were only asleep
But now that I know
You're in heaven happy at home
I guess we'll both
Be together always at heart.
It hurts
Knowin' I've seen
My father only twice
But through it all
You are always by my side

I saw the love in your eyes
How many more to go
I count one till number four
Maybe you'd be a star
But only God would know

Tearz all, through the year
Wonder when it'll stop
All the murder and killing, How many more

BUT OUT HERE I WIPE A TEAR DROP AND WONDER HOW MANY MORE

(THE POETIC SONG)

THE DREAM THAT WAS NEVER MEANT TO BE
Like the starz in the sky, we shine in the dark
Like the dawn of sunrise, we symbolize a hope in our hearts
I brush these tearz away, Accept the shame from pride
Sadly the day is buried in the night, But like the undying dream,
Witness the light shine bright, like the starz in the sky

There was once a land of heroes
Of joy, peace and love
Some were killed others separated
Into distant places
But the roots of these heroes
Grew stronger in the veins
Of this fallen race
My ancestors were made slaves
But we triumphed in vain
They tried to make us extinct
We were never meant to live
And when I woke from this painful dream (I realise)
I'm the dream that was never meant to be

UNTITLED

Am the run away man / And there'z nobody who could stop me
Envision my past / A life full of worriez
I came as a stranger / Not knowing who to trust
Maybe my life could be in danger / but am ready to run
I can't look behind / Sad picturez in my mind
Painful tearz az I cry / now am searching 4 a paradise
Emotionz flowing free / Az I'm rapping to the beat
Hoping to get some money cause we've all got to eat
Let me live
Let me cherish just another breath / live my life to the limit
And Prepare for my death.

UNTITLED

Stone wallz,
In my room,
Picturez of my heroez
And places that I hope to go.
Here I pause,
All alone,
A dream Iz all I have to give,
My life Is all I have to sing

Here alone,
BRIDGE: Looking out my window
The only thing that keeps me from the world
Here I sing
Cauze my pain don't matter at all.

Feel my pain, my criez embrace
CHORUS: Accept my shame, Just wanna make It through another day
And If I should die, and live you
All I pray, somehow you'll remember my face
Remember my name

I paused with you
tossed with you
And we would brag about Westi
Braggin' 'bout the day we'd make It
Now I'm alone
Smokin' pain away
Just hopin' you would be here
Am missin' how we use to be my peerz
Now take some time and
CHORUS:

FLY AWAY (PERFOREMED BY MOM)

Good-bye, my son,
Till we meet again,
But for now, just remember your roots,
Good-bye my son,
Till we meet again,
Though It hurts me, but I love you.
Good-bye my son
Till we meet again,
But only pain, will give me understandin'
Good-bye, my baby
I've got to hold on,
Let me cry, while you fly away.

FOR A MOMENT

For a moment, I held you close
For a moment, we shared some hopes
For a moment, we'd fantasize what we'd want in our funerals
For a moment, You sat right here next to me
For a moment, we breathed on the same dream
And for just a moment It gave you a cause to live
But in a moment, You were stolen into heaven
And it's hard knowing, all we shared was for a moment
And so I write this song, in memory of thoze moments

Just for a moment, you were like my brother
Handz holdin' on each other
Wishful thinkin' that's what we'd call livin'
On a sunny day from what we made
But I never had the touch
So you would always get much
Just for a moment

MADE OF YOU

Each time I curse they say that I lost my culture
Raized in a land full of western culturez
Dressed in jeans shiny chain so am named homie
Blamin' mama sayin' that she lost me
Can you blame me or sit back and call me crazy
Fantasiez and dreamz iz all that am chained in
Talkin' about that day when we'll ever make It
And how everythin' we ever saw would finally be our own
It waz hell from the first rap in Swahili
The ghetto came tryin' to make a straight shilling
From poverty and misery
They came and went from the troubles in the industry
Hopin' some day we'll see the light gleamin' in our eyez
Hopin' there'll be a time when we all rize
Make a tune am majorly confused
Blame the world am just made of you

CHORUS: Made of you am made of this world
Blamin' you am made of this world
Made of you just so that people can relate to me
Sometimez I try being me, but am just made of you

Livin' lavish seein' people runnin' at me
Fine women and ballerz beggin' for my autograph
And sometimes I wonder how long will this patience keep me under

AFRICA SHINING

Like the countless starz in the night
That give light in the darkness
And so are we starz
In the dark continent
And among the starz, one shines brightest
But also among the starz, one changes colour az It twinkles
Among us, there are starz
And in the vast dark land of Africa
These starz will shine the light into other nations.
Though I cry and give up on hope
My faith keeps me smilin' az I envision the day
When Africa will shine

I dreamt of a few shining starz
Comin' out of Africa
I dreamt of this dark land
Filled with light and happiness
I saw my people no more hungry
I saw the children no more dyin'
Saw diseases whirled inside a wind
I saw Africa shining

Africa shine oh!! Africa shining x 2
Lookin' at Africa, and I could see some shining starz
Shining so bright sharing their light Africa Shining

JUST HOLD ON

Hold on (We're gonna make It) x 2
I sit here, searching for hope, in my situation
Cryin' tearz, am alone, facin' complicationz
Iz there someone I could hold, someone to tell me where to go
This pain Iz diggin' deeper, tryin' to kill my soul
Sometimez I wish I could die, I feel nobody really carez
No more tearz in my eyez, Feel my hopeless prayer
Nobody recognized my trialz, No one heard my cryin'
I keep tryin', To give my loved onez, a hope to survive
I pray to God, But everyday still seemz hard
I put a smile on my face, I know someday I'll be a star
And when am gone, will anybody cry or mourn
Just sing this song, It's hard and I know, But hold on

CHORUS: Hold on (Just sing this song and don't you worry)
Hold on (You've got the courage so don't you worry)
Hold on (Be strong and remember my song
It doesn't matter what they say
Someday am gonna make It)

Sometimez, I feel a light in me
I feel It shine in me
So I do my best, To keep It shinin'
But just search your heart
Deep inside you, there'z a light in you
It's Jesus deep inside of you
So just…

CHORUS:

DIDN'T I?

Am telling Dear God, Please let me die
Wishing I wasn't born to live, this painful life
No one triez to see us, Even when we try
I refuse to be a dreamer
Knowing one day I'll be a star
Hoping God will make a way
So I never give up
Am on the bedroom floor
Composing a rap song
Emotionz flowing free, Am a rising rap star
And though they said I'll never make it
No one knowz about the future
I'll probably get paid
So many hopes, I can't be sure
But after the night And fading screamz in my mind
My hand on the mic, And you'll be singing my rhymez
Well Didn't I

CHORUS: Didn't I tell you that my day would come?
Didn't I tell you I would be a star?
Didn't I tell you I was gonna shine?
Well look at me now am rising to the top
Well Didn't I?

So I left you full of wonder,
You try to keep me under, but my heart wouldn't let
So I keep on going higher.
I came from the down low, led by my vizionz and hopes
Still no one knowz, How I made it to the top
They told me, stay in school and maybe you'll learn
But now the system iz a problem, It's getting too hard.

WE'LL MAKE IT THROUGH

Now I've been burstin' rhymez, through the tearz & smilez
All the while, Hopin' you could see me rize
I came a long way, all alone, trying' to blow
Being broke, made me choke, from the desperate hopes
Now you could love me or hate me, but am a dying breed
Filled with talent, but you take It, and am the one in need
I only tried to share the passion, of a musical dream
God forgive me for my actionz, am in pain, you see?
Wishin' the world understandz, The pain in a man
Again & again, despair seemz to dwell in my land,
Day by day, The terror of shattered dreamz haunts me
And If I never make It, will my family want me
Will I be another short comer, of jailed mindz
Will I ever make an album, to get to the top
And prove you wrong, some dreamz do come true
And If you feel the way I do, just chill we'll make It through

I'VE COME A LONG WAY TO WHERE I AM TODAY
I'VE COME A LONG WAY DOWN THIS ROAD TO FAME
I'VE COME A LONG WAY CHASING MY DREAMZ
DON'T KNOW WHERE THIS ROAD WILL LEAD ME TO
BUT SOMEHOW WE'LL MAKE IT THROUGH

FOR DEAD HOMIEZ

Nigga we done been through a whole lot of sh. together
From runnin' Westi to being down for whatever
And now that you're gone I got a whole lot of sh. to tell ya'
Thingz I should have said way back
When we were younger
Remember when we use to roll hand in hand
And now am trippin' on how I really miss you man
And remember when you and me would say
We'd get up out this hood and everything would be okay
It's all good now, we out the hood now
We had the same Ideaz, but not the same careers
We shared the same old laughs, but not the same tearz
You were my homie, my stoni, my rollie, my nigga
And never placed no sh. before me
Man, I swear to God I loved you for that
Why you had to get hit, where waz I
What time was It
You were supposed to get older with me
On stage handz on shoulders with me
Copyin' 'em range Rovers with me

And If It wasn't for the will that God had made
I'd turn back the handz of time and take your place
Sitting here trippin on how I miss you
Just thinkin' about what you meant to me my nigga
Even though your gone you will always be my nigga
Though made It "Home" am still missin' you my nigga
Am feelin' like the timin' waz wrong my nigga
Know you're smilin' dwon sayin' carry on my nigga
Sometimez my nights can get long my nigga
Sometimez I feel God did me wrong my nigga
So I had to write a song my nigga
Just to let you know that you're still my nigga

KEEP ON TRYIN'

Now az am walkin' through the dark street
Invasion of the moon light's my way az It's moon lit
Tragically az the rays pierce through my eyes
Strategically the night fades, think am goin' blind
I know am gonna make It, I feel the chains of despair breakin'
Tell my mama, shed no tear, I overcame my fearz
So check my story, explodin' while am unfoldin' this poetry
So lonely, victim of foniez, crooked crew'z, now my closest homie
Am stuck in the game, To hear the world scream my name
Want the fame, make some money, so I kik It in vain
Hear what I say,
Tomorrow'z just a memory of yesterday,
Till I die, I make the best of what I've got today

So how much more can I bare, am only to tryin' to rize
Pressure from the hataz, with their pryin' eyez
They watch my every move, plottin' how to stop my shine
Conversate, to eliminate me. They would rather see me die
Spit rhymes, so full of courage, embrace my rage
Am only real. It's how feel, as I burst on a page
I promised mama I would make It, I would never let her down
My satisfaction az a rapper, Iz just to make her proud
But man, It sure Iz hard, will I ever be a star?
I train, to perfect my rap game, I wanna live large
And from the dark, I roze, In search for the light
And even though sometimez I lose hope, I've got to keep on tryin'
I guess tomorrow'z just a memory of yesterday
I didn't achieve much, that's why I make the best of today

CHORUS: THOUGH I NEVER HAD A CHANCE TO RIZE
NEVER ACHIEVED MUCH YESTERDAY
GOT TO KEEP ON HOLDIN’ ON TO MY DREAM TIGHT
GOT TO MAKE THE BEST OUT OF TODAY
I’VE GOT TO KEEP ON TRYIN’

RAP

UNTITLED

Witness Interpretationz of my Intellectualness
Az I proceed to give you, understandin' of my life events
Truly, I beg the LORD, my soul to rest
Put me to death, euthanasia, az am bundled Inside my casket
devisionz, of my decisionz, man on a mission
taunted and haunted, coz of my own vizionz
conclusionz, up in a hearse
Wazn't It me, that spoke of dreamz, from when, I first burst
Injudicious hypocritics, fill the whole scene
Pozin' contemplate about my skill.
Waz I meant to make It, Look at me wishin;, and lost
Called crazy, ever since I spit out my thoughts
I'll be a star someday, Though am confined in a corner
of what I wanna teach, so I could die with honour
how much Ice may glisten, Just listen and change the world
This how It soundz when your caught, In the midst of thoughts
Pops waz never there to woop my ass & train me
Became my own man, so pliz don't blame me
Hate me now, Mama let me rip the crowd
I throw It down for my crewz, still chasin' the clouds 
I bump this one In the club,
Embrace my lessonz, pay attention, let me blow your mind
Crooked crew, my trusted older peerz
follow my lead, stay real, skill burstin' in tearz
They say am a grown man, They laugh, everytime I cry
But I can't understand, Coz I waz born to try
It gets harder, now wisdom, searchin' for in hunger
My thunder cripplez my foez, so they start to wonder
How will I make It, I keep on trying, It's a dream
Won't you roll with me, follow my team, scream my name

Lessonz, from the game.

REALIZE

You're a demonstrator of your mind & heart,
An action of feelingz into expressionz,
Opposing much of what others believe about you,
A reasoning of your own understanding.
You're assertive when you have to,
An Ingenious of expression,
You are your own leader against Injudicious men,
An unending struggler for sensible conclusion.
Satisfaction Iz a rare taste in your mind'z mouth,
And any wayz or meanz to get It,
Are your training groundz.
But you are also human;
Assiduous, but still human.
An achiever of unachievablez,
You are a winner of your like minded race;
Those who share in your vizion.
You have pain inside,
And rejection seemz to be a close friend.

Iz as an achiever's smile or a winner'z smile,
You are a factory of your own Idealistic Inventions,
Sparking the flame in your heart Into the mindz of others,
To embrace your thought.
You're a master mind of creativity,
You are your own judge of cause of action,
Your own witness to your destruction,
An acceptance of your own fiery nature,
As a sacrifice of others in despair.
You are unique, Thank God for your nature.

REBEL AGAINST IN MY OWN INABILITIES

I sauntered through a meditation,
In a journey to regain my lost spiritual peace.
Suddenly,
The peculiar, yet troubled youthful demon,
Caught up with me.
Attacking and Invading my heart, to which is manifestly
A prey,
It ripped out my Innocence and fear,
Ruthlessly Initiating me into a rabble of dreamerz.
The comfort of being with this like-minded "Race",
Consisting of philosopherz who were majority of overtones,
Caused deeper understanding & yearn for mind power.
My Inner eyez were open,
My mind welcoming mellifluous & wise literature,
That my tongue adapted to the linguistic Ingenius'
Of this demon, perhaps God given.
Gradually, I become obdurate,
Cold, when I realized that throughout, I waz solo.
Praying for euthanasia, coz the curse of loneliness,
Waz never evanescent in my heart.
But like the morning sun across my vast pride land,
I retaliated against my hurting,
Finding my soul deeply disturbed,
Stretched out and scattered against the conceding groundz,
Of fake love.
I was no longer appreciated and found no peace,
In listening to my heart's rhapsody.
It felt like retribution from the earthly gods,
So I ventured in hope, that someone might feel me,
Expressing the fury and experience in my tribulationz
So the world may embrace my vizion.
But as much as my skill waz viable, I had to throw it down.
Now I bump to the rhythm of my fearful & troubled heartbeat
In my quest for fame, as a rebel against my own Inabilities.

DON'T MAKE ME LAUGH

Burstin' my time up in the studio
Hopin' It'd pay someday
Accept my wayz I only need some pay
Sweaty head Greedy handz
Funny how the money'z got me so belly hungry
Cops runnin' upon me askin' for my Identity
I spit my name so full of hate
Az I say am Eddy
You ready check It ha!!
Am on a mission to makin millions
Envisionin' a better livin
Grievin' on homiez am missin'
Don't wanna die before I fly
Fast wheelz, A plush crib
Now can you dig It
Fine honey'z comin' runnin' each time I wanna hit It
Believe that cause yo!! am only dreamin
And you just don't know how much it eats me
Knowin' someday am gone make It far
Hopin' to be a star
Like Biggie and Pac
Once we part I hope to rest like a true legend
And you runnin' your mouth
Like you know what It's about
Truly doubt It
You just wanna cause a havoc
And If It wasn't for me
You'd never know how It feels
To be on the screen at only sixteen
Try looking tough cause now your living large
You don't know the half
Just don't make me laugh

BOUND TO DIE

My fate singing songs, until am barely breathing
Life is a prizon, Give me a reazon, why I must believe
My teary eyes, Look deep inside me, all I have Iz a childhood dream
Caress my pillow witness a star shining through my window
Blinded by the light shining through my dark nights
Mama pliz don't cry am only trying to survive
In time I know I'll make It Just keep the hope alive
Driven by tribulationz, my trialz, sometimes I wanna cry
Wonder why, It's hard to let, a young soldier fly
Searching for meanz, so I passive, To make It overseas
Let me unfold the story, of a dream that wasn't meant to be
Hoping you feel me, Hoping you'll always stay with me
Wishing you care, To be there, when am feeling scared
My every move is mandatory, will I be rocking
Before am buried or will I die so legendary
Coming from Africa this rap singer
Undying fantasiez into reality am tired of picturez
And even thoug I make It, will my people appreciate me
Embrace me from this life cauze am bound to die
Cause you know

It's hard for me to shine
In the middle of the night
Great starz shining bright
Overshadowing my light
In time
I know I've got to shine
I've got to keep on trying x 2
Even though am bound to die

HERE I COME

My lyrics explode, without a code, Az my feelings are shown
On my own, since I waz born. Let me share my cold
A spoken dream, unseen vizions, am trapped in a prizon
Desperate hopes, keep me alive. Look through my teary eyez
The nights, Bring out the light, Down, shining bright
Of a star, look up above, Let me feel the love
Prying eyez, I hear whispers, as am walking by
Dear people of mine, Am only out shine, Let me fly
Let's share the tearz, and the blood, and the sweat, of a struggle
Let my handz, serve az a sign, that my people got purpose
Feel my heart and embrace my pain,
Feel my wordz understand what am sayin'
Before am layed, To God I pray He'z gonna see us some day
Somehow, He'll make a way. Dear Jesus, can you feel me
If tomorrow comes, I hope I make It, Just to see the sun
Feel me now, az I burst, cauze here I come.

Suddenly I feel a rush az I anticipate
The whole place in a hush az I step on the stage
Beads of sweat streaming down my anxious face
I relocate the tense mood with thundering tunes
Soon am rapping az the whole crowd starts jumping
Without a worry my lyrics iz all my blood is pumping
Slowly flowing and I'm hoping I end up blowing
Mic I'm tight holding making G'z with the rhymes spoken
With poetry I tell a story of an endless dream
Was never meant to be and changed fantasiez to reality
Dreaming feeling bitter Got my legs feeling weaker
My head next to the speakers Az I bump to get It clear
Visualize a troubled mind It's not hard to find
Sometimes I wanna cry only wishing that I could die
Dear God look though my eyez, see my pain inside
Embrace me into heaven. It's hard, so here I come.

SONGZ OF FREEDOM

Captivity encircles the whole scene,
My life since birth, az I learned, Iz not worth living
Out of the gifted children, came out a fool from school
I guess am only real, cause you know what you've been through
I try express the way I feel, to a teacher
Quarellz then I win, then I got beat up
Now am stranded on my own, filled with questionz
How am I supposed to know you're not supposed to question
Oppression, authority enslaves us by rules
Expressionz of the truth now kill the youth
So If you feel me, I hope you're listening
We were never born free, look at all the killings
Take me Home Dear Father LORD
Am all alone trying to lead my people now lost
Mission for millionz, Father I beg for wisdom
Now my people, let's retaliate with songz of freedom.

I come out of a place, treated like a slave
Even though I tried, I waz still a young child
Nobody cared to ask me, why always cried
I pray to God, But I only cried out more
Soldier x 2 screamin' out "Westi for life"
African dream, This world waz never meant for me
Now take my hand, Just hold me now
Broke & helpless, I'm bound to go down
But you know, my heart is filled with hope
I smile a little more, singin' theze songz of freedom.
Songz of freedom, keep singin' through my head
LORD knowz I can't wait, Till the day I leave this place
Though I know, I know, am gonna miss your face
I know we'll meet again, in a better place
So now c'mon let's sing
Songz of freedom, Take me home.

MESSAGES FROM GOD

I AM

I AM,
Who I AM.
But who do they say
I AM?

But I say
I AM but Me.
Before Abraham was born
I AM.

I AM with you always
And none will ever love you
Like I do.
Rejoice,
And go to the Nations
To spread the good news.
For I AM
in you.

I AM

I AM
WHO I AM
But who do they say
I AM?

But I say
I AM but Me.
Before Abraham was born
I AM.

I AM with you always
And none will ever love you
Like I do.
Rejoice,
And go to the Nations
To spread the good news
For I AM
In you.

THE WORD

There'z a word
Being spread,
It's wonderful
And gives comfort,
Even to the dead.

The word was the beginning
And it was made flesh.
And now in Spirit,
In us, it tried to dwell.

The word
Iz the bread,
And the word
Iz life.
Know the word,
Learn the word,
Preach the word,
And live by the word.
And In accepting the word,
You have accepted God.
And in the acceptance of God
You have eternal life.

Be keen to listen
For it is being spoken.
Remove the wax
That deafens your ears.
Do not strain to hear
But again I say,
Be keen to listen.
For in hearing there is no understanding
Az Iz the opposite in listening.
Do not be cheated and go in search
Of the word.
For it is within you. Listen to your heart
And understand the word.

GONNA FLY

Came across a fantasy
After stumbling upon a dream
Az I escaped from reality
That only took the best of me
With eyez of hope
There I waz
A victim of not believing in realism,
My existence based on the fulfilment
Of all my endless dreamin'
Now can you feel me
Poetry lessons
To tell a story of my profession
My mind is an obsession
Witness the perfection of my rhymez
In due time I'm gonna fly

ANGEL OF MINE

I met a stranger
Who made me fly.
The stranger flew me away from my pain
Into a place of joy, love and no pain could be felt.
The stranger met me crying,
And wiped my tearz away.
Met me when I waz dying,
And blew out, the breath of dismay.
Found me sad,
And made me laugh,
Found me hopeless,
And gave me love.
The stanger'z armz,
Were gentle and warm,
But there waz more warmth,
That came embracing me from harm.
The stranger had wingz.

BLACK CHILD, SING

Black child,
Jailed mind,
In hunger, for some attention,
In anger, from caged expressionz.
Black child,
Brown eyez,
Trapped, in this world of liez,
Seeking, to express the thoughts inside.
Black child,
African born,
Silent criez,
And rapping a song.
With the heart of a warrior,
The rage is unhidden,
With simple words, that you may find meaningful,
He explores a dream, in him;
Listen; Listen to the black child sing.

I'm sitted here, trying to breathe, the air of freedom
I sing songz of my pain, hoping for retaliation
They tell me, I am free, but they abuse my rights
Don't you realize, that school rulez, jailed my mind
Blaming the law, The youth, can't even see God
Innocence is gone, when the cops, burst their gun shots
When will It stop. Did God bring us here to die
I live my life, with hopeless criez, And let It pass me by
Captured expressionz, So I passive to achieve from this profession.

THE GREATEST

Among the inferior
Stands one who is superior.
Among the unknown
Stands one who is to be known.

Among the humbled ones
Stands one who will be raised to glory.
Among the unseen,
Stands one with a vizion.

Among the poor,
There will be the richest.
Among the weakest
There will be the greatest.

Grateness is a priviledge
And to be great is an honour.
Among us,
Stands one who is to be the greatest.
The greatness is in you.

UNTITLED

Hunger stricken
Drought got him weakened
His belly hurting
Parents buried so no time for grieving
Living to see another day
By God's grace
Searching for a better way
Witness the pain in the child's face
And growing older
No hope for living
See him turned into a soldier
A master of killing
Only twelve years old
Witnessed his loved ones go
And shedding tearz no more
Now he's left all alone
And now the army
Iz his only family
So many shattered dreamz
Wondering If God's gonna punish him
For all hiz deedz
And in my mind,
I tried feeling the fear
So hidden deep inside
And uncontrollable tearz
As I start to cry
They tell me God haz a plan
For every one
So did He plan for this child
Just to grow and burn?

IF I HAD A CHANGE

Then many of whom claim to love me, shall only hate me
If I had a chance, to sit and talk to my mother,
Then emotionz would flow free, and I would only cry.
If I had a chance, to meet my father once more,
Then I would make him realize, just how much I need him
If I had a chance, to cry my pain and hurting out,
Then I would cry all my life.
If I had a chance to be happy,
And to know how it feelz to smile,
Then I would never want to die.
If I had a chance; just one chance,
I would want to be loved, like any one else.
To many, I put my trust, and to all,
I shared my poor heart with.
I gave each person a share of it.
It was clean, pure and sparkled like a star.
But when each person returned his share,
It was filled with dirt and was impure,
And my little star never sparkled again.
If I had a chance,
I would ask God to punish you,
But He has made me even love you more.
If I had a chance,
I would want to go home to live with my Father.
I would want to say I LOVE YOU with a pure heart
I would want Him, to kiss my tearz away
And to hear him whisper in my ear, “I LOVE YOU EDDIE.”
If I had a chance,
Then I would bring happiness to the world through He,
That is happiness; true happiness.
If I had a chance.
Then I would wish of this to be my last moment.

For no more pain can my heart endure.
If I had a chance,
Then I would love all forever
And only then, you will know, the true and everlasting love,
Shared unto me.
If I had a chance,
Then I would love to have the true and full anointing,
To preach, heal and bring back the children, to their Father.
If only I had a chance,
Then I would have wished to silence your mouths
For I listened to you, and am now in despair.
Mothers and Fathers, Traditions and Culture,
None shall ever be GREATER than the true I AM.
In obeying, I have learnt of the world
And what good iz it, to try and belong where you don't?
If I had a chance,
Then I would tell you all about heaven.
And if I had a chance,
I would tell you, of when I met God.
The Devil, comes in many ways,
But so does, the Glorious one.
I felt His presence, and so the tears,
How much He has loved me; How much.
If I had a chance,
The I would want to be held in the arms,
Of the person that I truly love.
And if she had a chance,
Then she may want me to hold her too.
I will love her, though I don't know how,
But I will truly love her, for she loved me first and taught me
I would heal, forgive and preach, only If I had a chance
If I had a chance, then I would cherish it forever.

LAND OF BLESSING

Land of blessing, Land of plenty
How fortunate you are, For you have gained God'z favour.
His presence fills the air, like no other Nation could compare
Like a marvelous strong building with a brick wall,
Your foundation Is based in the Almighty'z handz.
The fall of one brick, to you does not matter
But for we who dwell under are prepared to use that brick.
This is your destruction, Great Land of blessing,
For He who has blessed you, Is the one whom you have not appreciated.
Land of blessing, Land of opportunity
How ungreatful you are, To what God has done.
Injustice and oppression has covered your beautiful clouds,
And the great blue sky, has traces of sin.
Soon you and all that Iz around you will die,
As the air of sin shall cauze harm to the breath of blessings.

UNTITLED

It’s never too easy, But I know am gonna make it
African child get up, And don’t wait
Only God is gonna make a way
So don’t you stop, And listen to what people say
It’s a nightmare out there
But keep hoping for the better
I know you’ll find your dream out there
I see your tearz, And share the same fear
But it’s never too late, I know you’re gonna see your day
The pressures of this world, will keep you under
Only if you let them, keep on going higher
It’s a shame, so many went astray
Money and fame made the man what he became
A future so bright, I know one day you’re gonna shine
Let God be your light, And He will make you shine

LAMENTATIONS

There waz always something wrong

Too good, To be true.
Too deep. To understand,
Too young, To love
Too young, to understand true love.

Too Hazy, For the light
Too undeserved, To shine
Too young, to be a star
Too young. To shine like the light of a star.

They say I live in a fantasy,
Say, I breathe in dreams of fresh air,
But I must wake up to reality,
Cause the dream was never meant to be there.

Too young, To die
But you are too ignorant, and blind.
Cherish my wordz in songz, You'll miss them when I'm gone
But not too young to write this: There was always something wrong

THERES WAZ ALWAYZ SOMETHING WRONG

Too good, To be true,
Too deep, To understand,
Too young, To love.
Too young, to understand true love

Too black, For the light
Too undeserved, To shine
Too young, to be a star
Too young, To shine like the light of a star.

They say I live in a fantasy,
Say, I breathe on dreamz of fresh air,
But I must wake up to reality,
Cause the dream was never meant to be there.

Too young, To die
But you are too Ignorant, and blind.
Cherish my wordsz in songz, You'll miss them when am gone,
But not too young to write this; There waz always something wrong.

INSTITUTIONZ

Now who to blame,
The Institutionz?
The system of running the institutionz?
Or the people who control the system and It's function,
In the Institutionz?
We bare children,
We teach them most of what we know about life,
We Instruct them to learn the basics of life,
And be so ordinary as to take them to Institutionz,
To nurture their developing knowledge.
So tell me what It is all worth;
Fine, our seedz grew normal enough to speak like others,
And do things that would define them as humans.
But what Is It worth,
If he knowz all these things,
But considers himself a fool by judgement,
Of his abilitiez in the Institution?
We nurture the knowledge, o yes we do;
But what about a God given talent?
I tell you, If I was to base my future on Institutionz,
I would only be a hopeless dreamer,
Like refined gold that's only worth on this earth,
But useless in the Life after death.
I blame the power-minded-runnerz,
For the evident feeling of uselessness that has become of me,
Because the system, took much of my hopes,
And the Institution,

Became a factory of theoretical statues.
Practicalness means nothing to them
Because books took Its place.
No one will appreciate expression of truth,
The streets are only known to talk bullshit & gain remorse.
Institution: what you have done to me,
But I blame the runners of your system,
No one noticed our children's talents,
No one noticed what our children experienced through
Institutionz

WHERE'Z THE LOVE??

They taught me little Sunday school lessons
Hoping someday I'd be perfect
But gave no answerz to my questions
Now I find myself stranded.

They told me to obey my parents so as to live longer
But never told me about my talent.
I waz just a little younger,
Now I find the world taking me for granted.

But in growing I realized,
That the rich faces were smeared with smilez
Some said It waz only on the outside
But whether broke or rich you're bound to face pain inside.

They sent me to school to make friendz
But they later told me my friendz will take me nowhere
And at my temporary end
I found myself chasing dreamz through the air.

They told me do, and I did try
And when they said I did wrong, I tried to rectify
So I passive to reach my goalz, but my closest derailed my focus
And in their satisfaction I waz all alone, A joyful demonstrator but hopeless.
And so I asked the world "where is God?"

For they taught me that God is love.
Some said in your heart & others said up above
But check out my sinful heart, would God be there?
Where'z the love?

WHAT ABOUT THE PAIN

When I need ya' lovin' tha' most you were gone
And in a zone I woz solo alone, desperate state in motion
Cursin' the very blood, that you & I entangled in
Stranded, abandoned, in tha handz of another family
Imagine, put yourself in my shoez,
No-n to lose but ya' dreamz & ya' loved onez, told to chose
No one to listen to ya' heart, vizionz seen in tha' dark
Except fo' ya clique, krooked push you on to be starz,
Livin' hard, no more liquor at the bar
Come witness how me be super, flashin' roundz of poolerz
Mind elevated, through stages until my eyez dose
Life Iz hell without you nearby, am missin' you most
So what about tha heart, It turned cold
Tha love, so long gone, No No
But tha' hopes, still push on, till tha' day we meet again
All I wanna know, what about the pain?
Dear Mama,

Never saw my eyez at the birth of a child
And you my Father
All you ever gave a nigga, woz ya' hand on first sight
So what am I to do, for yearz I fought my hate for you
When I waz younger mama told me you'd come so I'd wait fo' you
Chillin' in tha sittin' room, Nites I cried
Sometimez tha' weight of pains too much, but still I try
Curiousity slow transformed, furious thoughts
Mad at tha' talent I possess, I progress no less
Either accept me az ya' son, but what about my in-lawz?
Keep It real Papa, ama still gonna spit raw
What about tha' love long gone, tha' rage I can't erase
Hold my face, feel my vibe, what about tha' pain?

OH MY LORD

TELL ME WHAT AM
LIVING FOR
POSITIONED IN DESPAIR
COZ THE WORLD
WON'T CARE

UNTITLED

What will It take,
For you to believe?
How long will tomorrow take,
While you grieve over yesterday?
How many more years shall pass,
While we struggle with reality?
How many more tears must I shed,
To make you believe in fantasiez?
Of what good are my expressions,
To a stone wall?
In the misunderstanding of my intensions,
I only meant to express my love.
Here I walk,
In the midst of friends & foes,
With words of scorn,
They have thrown in a mission,
To see me in a desperate position.
I live a fantasy,
Believe in miracles,
I breathe an air of oddz,
Relying on only God.
An African fantasy,
Iz a joke to other Nations,
Let them laugh,
Prove that you're mighty, over this reality.

SALE
'98 7 21

WHAT'S LEFT OF ME

What's left of me to do,
Now that there is no more hope in me,
What's left for me to do,
Now that am seeing the crushing of my dreamz.
What's the use of struggling,
When the oddz seem to be the mighty,
What's left to cry or try for,
Am hopeless, and only death seemz to bring comfort.
I try to be the best man I can be,
But no one appreciates me,
It's all over now,
And damn everything.
I was born alone,
My family Iz just me and my mother,
But does God really care,
He'z brought me shame and an undying despair.
So what's left of me,
When God doesn't love me,
What's left of my dream,
When I waz born in Africa
What's left of me,
When the only person I ever loved,
Could never give me a kiss.
What the heck Iz left of me,
Cauze I will die az nothing.
Just a useless black boy, regretting all the things I ever missed.
I told you a story about my dream,
I promised you that I would make it,
Now It's too late, I feel the strong wind of fate,
Coming now to take me.
My heart Is too fragile, But God doesn't understand
I don't want to go to hell, I was only dreaming.
You're all I have, I always hope you understand that.
The world never had time for me, now am dead, go and tell them about me,
And what is left of me.

UNTITLED

Perhaps my conversation, waz relatin', to ya' heart rate
Diggin' me slow, Don't wanna cauze you another heart break
Say you tired of men, claim, guyz are all the same
Though you stay, to let me hit you, with some more game
Ain't been long now, since I first met you around the hood
So down for ya' sista, I never noticed you
Didn't take much time, to pay you mind,
Though confessionz, I had you caught up in the corner of my eye
With the absence of ya' sista, she was soon in school now
It was all good, juz chillin' with you, foolin' around
And with time, affection, caught a brother unaware
Now am so lost in you, & I don't wanna play ya'
Coz I care, don't wanna treat you unfair, you don't deserve it
Shortie, I wanna be there, every you need, lovin'
Tight huggin' on cold cold nites, az we dream wild
And though my attitude'z shitty, I wanna do you right
Lookin' in my eyez, my pride, Iz all I got Inside
Only the realest, I roll with, You my true homie,
Hold me close, I'm feeling kinda low, kinda lonely
Lonely I sit, reminscin'
Contemplatin' on how we woz, & am missin'
All of tha' kisses & hugs, I don't mean to bug, Am in luv
With tha' garl, tha' fits tha' picture in my dreamz.
Baby Its you, Am in luv with you, Missin' you
Tha' way we use to kick It, me & you
How can I, say goodbye, to tha' luv of my life
Look in my eyez & tell me, do you love me still.

UNTITLED

I will avoid philosophizing,
But express philosophical thoughts,
In rhythm by song.

LETTERS TO GOD

Dear God,
I am afraid.
Afraid to live, and afraid to die.
I am afraid cause,
Nobody believes that you speak to me.
I wonder If It is really God,
Telling me these things.
Am a sinful man,
But you've promised me greatness.
I'm afraid,
Because all that people have said of you.
Is confusing.
I'm afraid to love and to hate,
Because you watch over me.
I'm afraid to look at the future,
For in the darkness of my sins,
It seems too bright.
I'm afraid to speak,
And I now feel weak.
I'm afraid to listen,
For I have angered them,
When I speak of your word to me.

DEAR GOD

I am afraid.
Afraid to live, and afraid to die.
I am afraid cause,
Nobody believes what you speak to me
I wonder If It is really God,
Telling me these things.
Am a sinful man,
But you've promised me greatness.
I'm afraid,
Because all that people have said of you,
Is confusing.
I'm afraid to love and to hate.
Because you watch over me
I'm afraid to look at the future,
For in the darkness of my sins,
It seemz too bright.
I'm afraid to speak,
And I now feel weak.
I'm afraid to listen,
For I have angered many,
When I speak of your word to me
Shall I be a hypocrite
Or shall they ask for a miracle.
I am only flesh and blood
Father Look at Me,
I'm only a man.
I'm scared of what may come next,
I'm scared for I do not hear your voice
Anymore
I am afraid to breathe,

For It could be my last.
I am afraid God,
I am afraid.
Look at your people,
Look at this earth.
Look at Me Father,
And look inside my heart.
You are creator and controller
Of all things great and small.
Control my heart,
And wash away my sinfulness.
Cleanse me and dwell in me
Forever more.
Show me a person
Who You have rested upon,
Let them speak your Word
And Let your word comfort me.
I'm afraid to sleep,
For I have one Dream.
Work in my dream Father,
And grant me no other.
Let my will rest in your handz,
As your will shall rest in mine.
Give me Courage and hope,
And Strengthen me wholly.
Wipe these tearz of fear,
And replace them with those of joy.
Fill yourself In me
And let me fill myself in you.
I ask for nothing,
But for that which you wish to grant me
I'm afraid, But though afraid,
You are still my strength and my all, Dear God.

HELP ME FATHER, HELP ME

They are with me, az I walk among them. They see me and speak to me for they have made me one of them. Through you, you have allowed me to indulge myself with what they do, and through you, you have granted me an eye and an ear to watch and listen, and learn more about them.

But you have granted me no tongue. You created me, and made You and I one. You speak to me and teach me and I have witnessed your amazing power.

You will punish these people, for they have angered you. You shall use the sun to make their skins dry and ugly. You will set free the diseases to consume them slowly but painfully and the taste of the bitterness of your anger, shall remain in their mouths az they die and will be passed on to the future generations.

But Father, you have laid me on the table of the earth like a cloth, and have let the cup of sin be drank upon me by the sinnerz. Each time they drink and a drop spillz, I am also drenched in the sin. Father, show me a loyal man with a tongue made of your word; show me a person made of your mouth.

His every word, shall be from You, and my every deed, shall come from Your loyal man. Show me a person who is rightful and righteous, and not a drop of sin, stains his flesh, soul, spirit, heart and mind.

You have given me the authority to witness, but Your warm love shared unto me, has resulted in I, loving those you wish to punish. Through eye and ear, and through your will, I will lead the one who is your mouth to preach and Your WORD, shall burn and pierce the flesh of man eternally, until sin is wiped off this Holy land.

Like in the time of Moses, I know that these people are stubborn Father and none knows more than You.

By your will unto mine Father, grant me Your Power, to conquer and to prove witness of Your existence, guidance and salvation. Let the loyal man not scream across the streets nor in Your Holy House.

Let Your guidance take us both through, righteousness and triumph over these people whom I have grown to Dearly Love, as my own. You have set free Satan and his allies, but Father, I plead in you, to hold back his rage, for man needs another chance with God the Father, the Son and the Holy Spirit.

I testify your word with my weak tongue, and these people have laughed and doubted me. I've been hurt and I have cried due to the weakness of my tongue Father. But with this prayer and hope, I come to You, For you are my help before I needed to ask for It. Dear God, Help me Father; Help me.

DEAR FATHER

I thank you for making me. I thank you for Eddie. I thank you cause of the dream. I thank you cauze of the vizionz. I thank you for a talent that I hope one day shall come to light; I thank you cauze this gives me purpose to live. I thank you for the fear, cause It only makes me more stronger, and I thank you for my enemies, I gain more from the lessons.

I thank you for the tearz, I have more reasons to smile, and I thank you for the anger, I get joy from happiness in you.

I THANK YOU FOR MY BOYZ, MY FRIENDS, they're my brothers and sistaz at heart for I have none by blood. I PRAIZE YOU AND APPRECIATE MY FAMILY, cauze when It's my turn to lead, I've got you're footstep traces in my dreamz to lead them to the right direction.

I thank you cauze your love haz made me love others. I thank you cauze God, you're my Father in heart, soul, mind, and strength. I thank you cauze I never had one here on earth, cauze he would never do the greatest thing compared to what you have done for me; the Fatherly Love to a child.

I know I sin, and that's why I'm not perfect, I know I suffer, and that's how I know I sin. My flesh deceives me and I may break all your commandments but one, "Love The LORD your God with all your mind, heart, soul and strength." Forgive me when I'm scared, for I will run, but accept me Father, for I run to you. Thank you Father for you have listened, thank you.

L*OVIN'* E**K**uria

BE REAL TO ME

They often speak of you,
And they oftenly praise you.
They tell stories of when you
Came to earth.
They say you died for us.
They say you're the creator
Of both great and small
They say you talk to your servants
Through vizionz and dreams.
They say you care.
And sometimes say that you don't.
They sometimes say that you're not there
But they still talk of heaven.
They say that you're just
And that all who live according to your word
Shall be judged fairly and receive eternal life.
But father,
Your houses have become,
The dwellings of hypocrites and evil minds.
Your house,
Is no longer a house.
But they still believe that you've blessed them.
They believe that you listen and reward.
I believe,
That not a single blessing befalls these.
Sin has consumed my flesh,
But my soul remains strong believing in the one true God
They tell me there's a heaven.
And It's where all good people go.

But show me one, who is worthy of heaven.
Show me one, that you have fully anointed.
Show me one, who your mighty hand rests upon.
They tell me, you're the King of Kings.
I pray to you, and believe that you hear me.
And sometimes I feel as though you speak to me.
Show me your glorious face.
Show me that It is the LORD.
That I speak to;
Show me you,
Be real to me.

DEAR GOD

I az a sinner through confession,
Approach you az a sinner.
Opposing death & hell
I proceed in bursting clear, tha' hearts speech.
I love my mother,
& I thank you for her meditation,
In understanding my thoughts.
Heal & protect her in thanks,
For tha' blessingz that prevail in her path.
Without much family,
I thank you for her succeed in trialz & tribulationz;
Her sacrifices from her heart,
To get tha' best outta me.
I am not worthy of much,
Though appreciative of tha' little I've earned.
I thank you for Shali,
Begging you to proceed our love into her being my wife;
Her being tha' mother of my child,
& for her never to leave me;
For me to tolerate her,
And love her deeper & more.
For our love to last through tests of time,
So we may be lovers of all time.
Thank you for her love & caring,
Be with us closely, I'm praying.

UNTITLED

Forgive me for my faults today.
Yesterday took most of my perfectness & Innocence,
So by tomorrow, I know I'll die a sinner.
Perhaps I was too real to live by my own principles,
Perhaps a sudden cautious thought saved me from falling,
I know through God's careful watching over me,
I will learn lessonz az I have.
Now am thrilled by my curiosity for wisdom,
To learn why I did this and not that;
Why should I base my future on education Institutes?
So much a fiery feeling in me burns deep,
Az Idealistic poetic thoughts eliminate theory teachings.
To base my life on practicalness is materialness,
And to base It on religiousness, Is unsureness.
So I base a fragile heart and sensitive soul,
On a dream, believing that It is God given.
With both practical & religious tastes,
My spirit has become powerful,
And my mind has gained tremendous understanding.
My eyes have excavated through books & teachings of philosophical genius',
And I have concluded myself, a genius of my originalities.
Most say I don't care, and based my future,
on their own predictions.
Basing my future on my attitude towards the approach
of my hearts fulfilment,
I have experienced the zest of my spiritual Intellectualness
Thus, I'm cautious not to emulate yesterday's faults
Coz It will kill my realness.
But the endogenous of expression, still swims in my heart
And wrong Interpretationz have enslaved me in sin.
So now I chill in solitude for after repentance is temptation.
Test not my fragile heart LORD,
Until the full understanding of wisdom and experience in courage
Is encapsulated in me, so as to face tomorrow.

DREAMING

Must have been a dream
But somewhere in my mind
Waz a thought trying to break free
An expression of my feelings
Will I ever make it
Only time will tell
And all that's in my head
Iz the flames of hell
Am slowly burning down
Slowly crumbling down
Hold me now
Show me the meaning of love, see
I don't want your mercy
Am getting so weak
And I can barely walk
Just when am starting to rise
That's when they wanna talk
They say my death is close
Am living fast
So they compare it to a rose
The petals falling with my every breath
So am begging God
Help me see another day
It was never meant for me
To be this way am trying to change
My lyrics expressing all
My deepest feelings
I wanna make it to the top
Have a couple of millions
The Industry's dead
And so we all grieving
I wanna cause a change
Or am I still dreaming

DON'T PASS-BY MY DOOR.

Don't pass-by my door, Dear LORD,
For It is painted at the top, with the blood of my pain.
Don't pass-by my door,
For I have awaited your salvation, in vain.
Save my dream the only thing that's mine.
Save my family, the only thing I have.
Destroy those that have hurt and punished me,
For in punishing me, they have punished you.
Restore my broken heart, and bless my home
Do not destroy that which is weak, Don't pass-by my door.

DEDICATIONS TO MY MOM

Dear Mom,

I guess I couldn't tell you this by face so I chose to put It in writing. With all my deepest appreciation to God for you and all you've been through to get us here, I guess you were always right.

Right now I think, looking back at where we started and where we are, but to tell you the truth, I wish we could return. I wish we could go back to being simple and humble as we were cause this life was surely never meant for me.

It's hard keeping up the pace with the richibility cause I belong to the innocence and guilt of my simple beginnings. That's why I wish I could erase the hopes and dreams cause that's what got us here in the first place.

Mom It hurts cause, when I make you mad I feel worthless. I'm the reason that left you in the reason we're here. When people are mad and hurt cause of me, It's deep cause you bore me a sufferer and a struggling child.

Am your only baby, but the rejection is far beyond what I can endure; I'm too superstitious and deep in my religion. Some see me and judge me by what I do or who I love. Mom, God doesn't take the good people to heaven and sometimes I don't understand God.

Why does He let me feel pain If He cares so much? I wish you never gave birth to a hopeless creature and shame of creation like this. I wish I was an angel; I'd make sure you came to heaven, I love you too much.

But I'm a dreamer, always waking up

DEAR MOM,

I guess I couldn't tell you this by face so I chose to put It in writing. With all my deepest appreciation to God for you and all you've been through to get us here, I guess you were always right.

Right now I chill, looking back at where we started and where we are, but to tell you the truth, I wish we could return. I wish we could go back to being simple and humble as we were cauze this life was surely never meant for me.

It's hard keeping up the pace with the rich kidz cauze I belong to the innocence and guilt of my simple beginnings. That's why I wish I could erase the hopes and dreams cauze that's what got us here in the first place.

Mom It hurts cauze, when I make you mad I feel worthless. I'm the reazon dad left you, the reazon we're here. When people are made and hurt cauze of me, It's deep cauze you bore me a sufferer and a struggling child.

Am you only baby, but my rejection is far beyond what I can endure; I'm too superstitious and deep in my religion. Some see me and judge me by what I do or who I look. Mom, God doesn't take the good people to heaven and sometimes I don't understand God.

Why does He let me feel pain If He carez so much? I wish you never gave birth to a hopless creature and shame of creation like this. I wish I was an angel; I'd make sure you come to heaven, I love you too much,

But I'm a dreamer, always waking up to the harsh reality of living. I'm lonely and without a brother or sister whom too many of my friendz brag about.

But your're too caught up in accomplishments and I want you to shine. I wish that sometimes I could hold you and cry and sleep while I'm lying on your laps. I wish you could say "I LOVE YOU" and tell me I've done something good; I wish you would understand, but I blame this reality.

I miss saying when you would come back from work, and If you would even come back from any other place.

I cry az I write this letter cauze mom, I miss yesterday, but today has taken over, so I can only hope in prayer for the best, when tomorrow comez.

I LOVE YOU

I **L***OVE You'* **A**lwa'z E**K**uria

CAFE
POPCORN

LET MY FLY (TO MAMA)

Through the storm and through the cold,
You have kept me warm az you've been bold.
In the palms of your struggling hands,
You have kept me under the protection of your love.
We've not only shed tearz, and shared the joy of a family,
But also love and blood.
So many sweet things you've done for me,
Your sweat Iz an undying blessing.
But in the palms of your strong yet tender hands,
I have looked around and found that am alone.
I am your only baby, the only thing you cherish.
But az I look up, I see a most shinning star on top of me
We've shared the dream and someday I will fulfil It.
You have given up your life, and countless things for me,
Though I am your only true joy, someday you must also give up, me.
Keep on smiling, No need to cry.
So long as that star keeps shining, my spirit is still alive.
I will love you always, and keep you special inside.
So much I must accomplish, for It is God's work;
For In your handz I lay, and In His hands you lay.
I know It's hard, and now is the time,
My spirit dwells in your heart; Let me fly.

LOVIN' Alwa'z EKuria

UNTITLED

If there'z a chance for me to come home
Pliz mama, open up the door, now am grown
Let It be known, I suffered long enough, moths on end
If there'z a chance, let me feel ya' love, once agen.

Caught unawarez, by the grip of drama, at an early age stressin' mama
Thinkin' the world would care, a victim of life's traumaz
Once mama left, in the dark zone, I was all alone
Dedication to Isolation.
Mind stationed on medication, like am up in prizon
Vizionz in form of hallucinationz,
Livin in my position, you would probably cry
Mama gone, & don't know Papa, though he probably died
And at the birth of a dream, lost in pursuit of G'z
Trialz consumed by the fury flamez of misery
Roze up alone & I know ain't no one like Jamo,
& your homie out in Westi
Ain't made It, but wear tha' payback sure crazy
So peep my poetry, stories, proceedin' with no end
All am askin', let me feel love, your love once again.

Should I deny the fact I miss you
Wishin' that I woz still with you
Missin' you most, how we rolled
Tattooed my soul, wich ya' thoughts
And how we woz, could not possibly be defined right
Forgive me mama, I woz chasin dreamz on latenites
And in the midst of ya' earz, I told you promises
Though It's clear, your son so dear, never accomplished 'em
And though daddy, you gave me a handshake on first sight
embrace the feelings of ya' lonely child
made a bond with niggaz I use to love, up above you,
put no one else through this life of hell

UNTITLED

There'z a lady on the scene
But oh! Can't you see her?
There'z a lady on the scene
Causing the most painful hurting and deepest joy.
There'z a lady on the scene,
But oh! Now you don't know her?
She'z simply herself and in her own nature,
Damn! It's your mother.
Check out the lady on the scene
Accepting the painful whip of shame and struggle beat her.
She'z only doing her best, to keep providing for you.
Damn! I cherish the tearz, blood and sweat.
There'z a lady on the scene,
Who never threw me away to die coz I may have been a burden
She raized me, not knowing,
Soon an unexpected talent, would grow to a passionate dream.
Damn! Many must wish they were her
Check out the pride of my mama,
From the shame, I appreciated her struggle & turned her to a star
So now do you see the lady on my scene?
It's sad! The fame came after so much hopelessness.
Embrace the pain, Embrace the struggle,
Embrace the care and acceptance when you were up & down,
Embrace the passion of the deepest love
Go on, Embrace Dearest Mama.

RUN BABY RUN

Run baby run, cause here they come,
Run baby run, Before they take my only son.
Let the wind from the east, blow you into the west
Keep alive the endless dream before they take my breath.
Run baby run, express the courage in your spirit,
Run baby run, I know you're scare, but won't give in.
Though your actions, have scarred my heart,
You've made me learn, That there'z a star, through your words.
Run baby run, and please don't turn back.
Brave the pain, For your soul, never down will It let.
Excel in your abilitiez, use them to the fullest
For though they may capture me keep watch for the bullets.
You're my breath. You're my heart.
And only death, could pull us apart.
I love you, and I need you to be strong,
And though I may wish to relieve the sound of my baby's songz,
There'z time for everything; For now, Run baby run.

I OFTEN CLOSE MY EYEZ

Captured in a fantasy from this painful reality,
Am swept in an ocean of peace and an air of dreams,
In a place called eternity.
Though cruel It may sound, I'm kidnapped into gentle armz,
Where happiness lays all around, and the feeling of true love, hold me firm.
The fleshy and juicy fruits of wise yet deep words,
I eat, to overcome the hunger of foolishness in defeat.
It's a passion, that comforts me when I cry,
And a hope for the better, when I have failed from trying.
Though my hurting deep inside, Is dismissed by my smile,
To hide the tearz and all my pain, I often close my eyez.

UNTITLED

Born hungry
Raized without a daddy
Mama, come rescue me
Reciting on my life story
How they use to laugt at me
Day by day
Waz just another family tale
Waz hell
My friends speaking
About their daddy'z
Feeling unworthy
So hard to tell
How It came to this
Till the day I fell
A victim of my own misery
Look to the starz
So high up above
Searching places so far
Hoping for a fatherly love
Hoping you know me
Embrace my story
How I grew so lonely
Mama I'm calling
Won't you hold me tight?
Feeling alright
In time I know I'll understand
When I'm finally a man
Just take my hand
Lead me through the right path

UNTITLED

And in my mind
My only purpose is to make it
Vizionz of a better life
Though they say am crazy
Mam'z slowly loosing her baby
He wants to be a star
His eyez set on the price
Hoping to live large
Don't shed a tear
The LORD help you eaze your fearz
I feel my dawn drawin' nearer
So It's not too far
I'll be a star

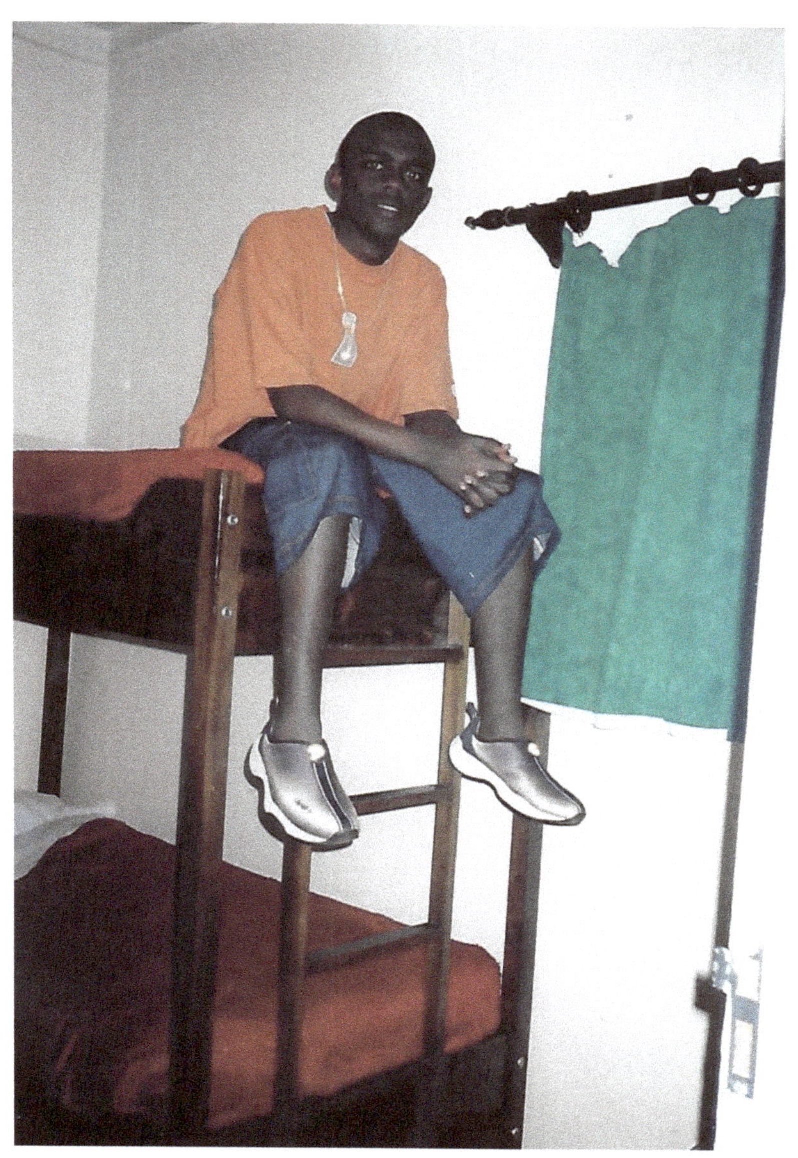

AS IF ITS ALRIGHT

As If It's alright,
We better wake up to the facts of life
Time to realize
That someday we're gonna die
Be examples to the children
And we should all learn to listen
Your baby haz got a vizion
Try to give him some attention
Lessons from all the mistakes
Can you relate?
Criez over corruption
While we sit, Time to take some action
Make a responsible lady
Out of your poor baby
From a boy now a man
Grown up with no father figure
We say money's the root to evil
While we killing our own people
Just trying to survive
As If It's alright

THE WILL

The will

There's a will which I must ffulfil. Understand the true meaning of what I say. For I truly know, that there's a will. There's an emotion burning to be spoken out, there's a teardrop, fforming in my lonely eyes.

Now, the teardrop, shall express my deepest emotions, and the emotions shall set ffree the true will, which I am to ffulfil.

In so much sin, I have been blinded, my fflesh is weak, and the painful lashes of this earth, have scarred, my heartless heart, It is not ffit to be a heart, ffor that which may make it so, has been stolen and taken away ffrom me.

It's hard to say that I love you ffor which love, have I been shown? For those that I have loved, have shown me none, so each time I pray, that someday yes, someday, I will hear this words before I die.

My body is destined ffor ffate, and destruction eagerly awaits. I have hurt many, who cared ffor me and some, still do. Now, I am a man like anyother. I do not prophecy, but the word, dwells in my heart. I will not be held back ffrom telling many and to all people, about the word. It is life everlasting, it is the bread of life, It is the Lord Jesus Christ.

Mourn not over me, nor shed a tear over me, ffor In the word, dwells the Holy Spirit. Rejoice all over the world, ffor a time is coming, when I will be ffilled with the anointing power, and all, shall receive the word.

Give your hearts to God, lift your hands in praise. His spirit is sent and dwells in the saved and behold, the body is destroyed but the soul forever stands indestructible and in the soul dwells the WORD and in the WORD there shall come true salvation.

At the top of the highest mountain, and in the deepest valleys the WORD will be forever proclaimed. Come down from the highest points, and rise up from the lowest. Gather around with your hands lifted high above to the Great King the true Messiah and everlasting God. Honour His presence and believe in the WORD. Gather around all the world, open your hearts for His presence will be welcome to every open door.

I see the children in a war, now happy as they play. I see the old, joyful as they spread the WORD. I see the lame run in every direction with their hands lifted up to heaven for they are healed.

I see the dying walk out of their hospital beds and some crying for the WORD overcomes death. I see an unchanged world, but a changed people who belong not to this world but to their Father up in heaven. I see the poor, now rich in Spirit, I see the lonely happy, for their with Jesus by their side. And I see God's glory rise in the hearts of all, as the sun rises by the great Oceans.

Praise Him all the world. Sin is overcome for I see each one of you in the Glorious Kingdom of Heaven. I see the blind with their eyes wide open as the wonders of the Father take place. If I die before this; before sight of this, then I have failed my duty. May the WORD live forever and when or this has happened, then I shall have fulfilled His will. May His will be done

THE WILL

There'z a will, which I must fulfil. Understand the true meaning of what I say, for I truly know, that there'z a will. There'z an emotion burning to be spoken out, there'z a teardrop, forming in my lonely eyez.

Now, the teardrop, shall express my deepest emotions, and the emotionz shall set free, the true will, which I am to fulfil.

In so much sin, I have been blinded, my flesh is weak, and the painful lashes of this earth, have scarred, my heartless heart, It is not fit to be a heart, for that which may make it so, has been stolen and taken away from me.

It's hard to say that I LOVE YOU for which love have I been shown? For those that I have loved, have shown me none, so each time I pray, that someday…yes, someday, I will hear this words before I die.

My body is destined for fate, and destruction eagerly awaits. I have hurt many, who care for me and some, still do. Now, I am a man like any other. I do not prophecy, but the LORD, dwells in my heart. I will not be held back from telling many and to all people, about the LORD. It is life everlasting. It is the bread of life, It is the LORD Jesus Christ.

Mourn not over me, nor shed a tear over me, for In the WORD, dwells the HOLY SPIRIT. Rejoice all over the world, for a time is coming, when I will be filled with the anointing power, and all, shall receive the WORD.

Give your hearts to GOD, lift your hands in praise. His spirit is sent and dwells in the soul and behold, the body is destroyed but the soul forever stands indestructible and in the soul dwellz the WORD and in the WORD there shall come true salvation.

At the top of the highest mountain, and in the deepest valleys the WORD will be forever proclaimed. Come down from the highest points and rise up from the lowest. Gather around with your friendz lifted high above to the Great King the true Messiah and everlasting God. Honour His presence, and believe in the WORD. Gather around all the world, open your hearts for the presence will be welcome to every open door.

I see the children in a war, now happy as they play. I see the old joyful as they spread the WORD. I see the same run in every direction with their hands lifted up to heaven for they are healed.

I see the dying walk out of the hospital beds, and some crying for the WORD overcomes death. I see an unchanged world, but a changed people who belong not to this world but to their Father up in heaven. I see the poor, now rich in spirit. I see the lonely happy, for they are with Jesus by their side. And I see God's glory rise in the hearts of all, as the sun rises by the great oceans.

Praise Him all the world, sin is overcome for I see each one of you in the Glorious Kingdom of Heaven. I see the blind with their eyes wide open as the wonders of the Father take place. If I die before this; before a sight of this, then I have failed my duty. May the LORD live forever and when all this has happened, then I shall have fulfilled His will. May His will be done.

GOD BLESS ALL

PREMONITIONS

WHEN I CLOSE MY EYES

When I cloze my eyez, I know
Someday I will die, I'll be gone
When I cloze my eyez, I feels good
Emotions as I sing, to you
And when I cloze my eyez, am in a fantasy
Escapin' from the pain, of reality
So even when I die, Don't you cry
Am in a place of peace, when I cloze my eyes

WHEN I CLOSE MY EYES

When I close my eyez, I know
Someday I will die, I'll be gone
When I close my eyez. It feelz good
Emotionz as I sing to you
And when I close my eyes, am in a fantasy
Escaping from the pain of reality
So even when I die, don't you cry
Am in a place of peace, when I close my eyes

MY LAST DEMISE

In sadness and joy
I hope to be remembered,
After my last breath
When no more of me, will there be ever.

With every move I make,
With the sight of another day,
I cherish it all
And give God, all the praise.

And in my friends,
And my peerz,
Each moment that we share
Always endz up in tearz.
You are all like my brotherz
And sisterz that I alwayz hoped for
I loved you all, like no other,
And hope you will too, even after am gone.

Let me live like any other man
Die, like any other man,
But be remembered,
Like no other man.

And if am to die,
At the prime time of my life,
I thank all who've been there for me.
And if for me you are to cry,
May I be a memory
In my last demise

THE EYEZ OF EXPERIENCE

I've not seen It all,
But seen all that my life would let me.
I've not been through It all,
But I done been in It.
My searching eyez dismiss my Innocence,
Coz am guilty of chasin' my dreamz.
My eyez ashy & grey aged,
Are Framed within the wallz of pain & trialz,
Ancient hopes cultivated,
I've fought a wasted battle, still dreamin' in denial.
Facing each day az If It was yesterday,
I saw tomorrow in my vizionz,
And though I knew It was a burden,
I'm pain addicted & had to face life az planned.
I've seen too much;
I musta seen It all,
And when I cry,
Joy iz reborn in me through the wonder of how I brave tomorrow.
I knew It was comin',
Soon as the dawn woz conceived,
I relieved the pain again & it woz more intense,
But I woz much wizer to handle it through the eyez;
The eyez of experience.

IN THE EYEZ OF FOREVER

So much I hope to achieve
So much a star I seek to be.
So many dreamz I hope to fulfil
So much glory, I hope to see.

The vizionz have led my path,
And I hope to make them real,
Before my death.
I am ready to suffer
For this is all that matters.

In my life,
I hope to do, not what you feel is right,
Nor what I feel iz right,
But to do what's right,
According to Christ.

I shall cry,
But never be ashamed.
For I believe inside
All this pain shall once be changed.
In all the pain and sorrow,
Through it all
There'll be a brighter day to follow.

Though the shower'z of sin,
Try to flood what I believe,
Never shall It's waters cover
The truth in my heart.
For I see
Through the eyez of forever.

L*OVIN'* E**K**uria

UNTITLED

In my brain cellz, you'll prevail in form of memoriez
When I die
And to the clique, how I love you, we made It through the struggle
Well equipped to get a G from how we hustled
And hope the world will embrace us to elevate us then
Study the breath I exhale, If I die, my love dwellz

UNTITLED

And the clock keeps tickin'
Minute after minute
And all that's in my mind'is an end to my livin'
Figure It'll bring more joy
It's like am living just for fun
Never a chance to be a boy
Cauze life
Show me no smile and so I cry
This cruel world's taught me
To live is like to die
I keep on Dreamin'
Tell me when my day iz comin'
and all my life to the grave
I hate those who love me
They say they understand
And so
They won't listen
Lord set me free
From this hell in prison'
A man can judge
The life of another
Wonder who's incharge
Let's love one another
Every breath I cherish
Wanna make my memory'z
For those who've perished
They're in heaven away
From this life's worrriez
And through it's not too far
I know I'll be a star
For I believe in my heart
And so I never give up

MY HOPES AND DREAMS ARE STILL ALIVE

So much I hope to shine,
So hard it seemz, and so I cry.
Lonely tearz of pain, soak my bedsheets
Wonder if there'll ever be a day
When I'll finally make it.

On my kneez to God, I give Him my whole
But it hurts, when I realize that am still alone.
Will I never have a father, in heaven and earth?
A life of loneliness and pain, has prevailed in me since birth.

My heart aches, And my strong walls of hope,
Await to be broken, by the shattering waves of these life's ocean
A final tear drop, streamz down from my lonely eyez
Slowly I brush it away, my hopes and dreams are still alive.

LOVIN' EKuria

IN THE WAKE OF TOMORROW

So many paths, I hope to follow,
Fulfil my all before death, so that I may rest in comfort.
The sun shall rise, and it'll be my day
And so will I, struggle to be great.

My poetry of love, I share with you
And my wealth of hate, I have fallen into
So much joy, I hope to bring before I die,
And every moment with you, I'll cherish before my last goodbye.

Do not drown in sorrow, when I am finally gone
I know you will be happy, in the wake of tomorrow.

LOVIN' EKuria

TELL THEM I AM FREE

Though they see me in chains of all oddz against me,
Tell them that my spirit, has overcome captivity.
Though my eyez have been blinded by the dust of your hopeless words
Tell them my mind is fresh filled with hopes, and faith in my heart.
Though they may try to kill, my endless dream
Though I may die, The dream is still alive.
Though they may starve me, from food or drink,
Tell them that I feed, on a God given dream.
Though I may be alone, God is always with me
Tell my people not to worry, Great things are to happen.
And though the strong walls of hate and anger, look down on me
    Tell them I have a bright star; Tell them I have an angel,
    Tell them that I am free.

MY STORY TO TELL

Here, I sit alone, Trying to compose myself
With words of passion, here'z my story to tell.

LOOK AT ME!! I'M ONLY A MAN

Do not be blinded by material things,
Do not be cheated In believing they make you happy.
Do not be blinded into giving me praise
For though many may see my face,
And though many may scream my name,
I was never born into fame; fame grew into me.
Give praise to God, the giver of the dream and all else
So Look at me!! I'm only a man.

REMEMBER ME

Remember me ("The Boys")

In all the things I do
Both the bad and the good
I hope to be remembered
Even though I may have hurt you

I lived to be cherished
And for those I may have hurt
I beg for your forgiveness
And hope to be special once more in your heart

Remember me
Not because I was crazy
But for I was human deep inside
Till the time of my untimely demise

In being known
You'll be remembered after you're gone
And so shall I strive to achieve my goals
In doing what I do right
And to be remembered after my last goodbye.

Life is a chance to live
And to live is a chance to cherish life
And so will I cherish each day that I live
For after I am buried
I will only be a memory
Remember me.

REMEMBER ME (THE POEM)

In all the things I do
Both the bad and the good
I hope to be remembered
Even though I may have hurt you.

I lived to be cherished
And for those I may have hurt
I beg for your forgiveness
And hope to be special once more in your heart.

Remember me
Not because I was crazy
But for I was Edwin deep inside
Till the time of my untimely demise.

In being known
You'll be remembered after you're gone
And so shall I strive to achieve my goals
In doing what is right
And to be remembered after my last goodbye.

Life is a chance to live
And to live is a chance to cherish life
And so will I cherish each day that I live
For after am buried
I will only be a memory
Remember me.

UNTITLED

Do I have a place
In heaven or hell
Well, each day
I beg the Lord
To help me change my sinful wayz
And in my prayer
Am on my kneez
Begging pliz
Knowing that he carez
Before I rest
I hope to be a better man
Never had a chance
And I hope He'll understand
Let me cry
But later feel the joy
It's hard to even try
After my life az a boy
Make a couple of G'z
And move my mama to a new house
Prove that all my dreamz
Would once make her proud
It's hard to be the best
An African dream
A young child
Trying to make it
Remember me
If I make it to the big screen
And if I die
I hope you never forget me
It's not a lie
Look into my eyez
See the star deep inside
I wanna shine bright
Before my last goodbye

UNTITLED

In my last goodbye
Remember my words
In my final resting place
Remember what I said
In my final view
Remember what I said to you
My last wish, Before am in peace
Remember the dream,
And the God who brought us here
Nothing in the world was made to be mine,
So I never came to get what's mine

HERE I LAY

The fears that you face today,
Brings the courage of tomorrow,
The tears that are shed today,
Eazens your sorrows.
The bullets of the night
Bring sadness to sparkling eyes
The taste of death
Is bitter, and causes us to cry.
This life we live,
Is only but a chance,
For we are bound to eternity,
Together up in heaven.
The smile on your face
Iz a memory that cannot be replaced,
The warm, yet wise words you said,
In my head are always replayed.
And now I tell you,
Here I lay; a dead corps
Though am dead, my dream won't stop;
Here'z the vessel, with the one brightly coloured roses.
For a moment, you embraced the fragrance,
Yet for a moment, I was treated like a stranger.
Here I cry, az this letter I write,
Of poetry that you might,
Remember me for, when I die.
A bright star once shone in the sky at night,
A bright light gleamed in these teary eyez of mine.
For a moment, I gave you a beautiful noise,
And for a moment, You heard my voice.
Let the courage in my brave heart be expressed
Let the spirit of my fiery soul be seen in my distress
I fight to live a life that I wish I could die in, to conquer death
Here now, I take my last breath az I pray; Here I lay.

THE FUTURE (IT GETS FURTHER)

I breathe rhymes, Every other day
Making my pay, to stay alive, I've got to lead ma' life
They tell me that am a dreamer, They'z no way am gonna make It
Believin' that there'z a Jesus, Hopin' for a better way
My pain, is never endin', and am tredin' on despair
Check It, I'm chasin' dreamz, through the hopeless air
Imagin', a rhyme breather, az I make your body shiver
Talent believer, am burstin just a rap singer
And even though, I never blow
Some how I know, somebody out there'll appreciate my flow
I know, some may be thinkin' am a crazy kid
All alone, I know am gonna make some crazy G'z
Till I die, I hope to rize, determination in my eyez
In time, I know I'll fly, so I breathe theze rhymez
To the youth, remember me, And don't you ever hesitate
Tell the truth, az you believe It, cauze the future won't wait.
IT GETS FURTHER, AS I CHASE MY DREAMZ
IS THERE A FUTURE, FOR US
I BREATHE ON THEZE RHYMEZ, I KNOW I'LL BE A STAR
JAILED EXPRESSIONS, UZE YOUR TALENT, THE FUTURE WON'T WAIT
IT GET'S FURTHER

FAMILY STORM

FAMILY STORM

I must admit, she had me fury driven
Sinkin in evil scheming; just a product of my [illegible]
Thinkin of freedom, victory has been a part of me
This heart of mine, a world of [illegible], so [illegible]
The [illegible], no one was there for me, but [illegible]
Part of my past, a full blast of my present story
A chill in solitude & tears trace upon my face
[illegible] to [illegible] [illegible] my heart & [illegible]
[illegible], my [illegible] calm the flames [illegible]
[illegible] [illegible], but you are [illegible]
[illegible] [illegible] [illegible]
[illegible] [illegible] [illegible] my blood
[illegible] [illegible] you [illegible] your own [illegible]
To keep [illegible] your [illegible] still I [illegible]
[illegible] a shame. God damn. I made him more of a [illegible]
[illegible] disrespectin me, you turned your nephew into a [illegible]
[illegible] in a sense, [illegible] presence [illegible] by the [illegible]
I bet you [illegible] every detail that you [illegible]
[illegible] of twisted minds, befalls the family
[illegible] in silence, [illegible], can't barely [illegible]
[illegible] a prison, [illegible] visions of my memories [illegible]
[illegible], the only [illegible] [illegible] [illegible] gets
[illegible] look at you with eyes of pain, [illegible] revenge
[illegible] back [illegible] the hands of that [illegible]
I leave this here [illegible] teach you; family storm

FAMILY STORM

I must admit, she had me fury driven
Sinkin in evil scheminz; just a product of my sinnin'
Thinkin' of freedom, victory has been a part of me
This heart of mine, a world of fight, so mama, pardon me
The Agony, no one was there for me, but misery
Part of my past, a full blast of my present story
I chill in solitude & tearz trace upon my face
No one to talk to, so my heart & rhyme soon relate
Beat laced, my instrumentalz calm tha flamez u cause
Memoriez, angered by what you are & what you waz
Or what I thought you waz,
Couldn't fully trust my own blood
& Even worse you hate your own coz now I'm grown up
To keep It real, your son is twenty one, still Immature
It's a shame, God damn, I made him more of a man
In disrespectin' me, you turned ya' nephew into a menace
& in a sense pretence uncovered by my momz absence
I bet you twisted every detail that you preached of me
& now a race of twisted mindz, befallz the family
I moan in silence, late nites, cant't barely cloze my eyez
It's like a prizon, seein' vizionz of my mama'z smile
& That's the only joy her baby boy so rarely gets
I look at you with eyez of pain, plottin' revenge
Stay back & pay back iz in the handz of the LORD
I leave this here, & let my wordz touch you; family storm

UNTITLED

Dreamz to glisten, Imprrizoned by the blood of my own
Meditated, upon escaping, this slavery of my thoughts
Paused & contemplated a plot in my brain cavity
activity to enable me, outta misery
Will God forgive for me killing the Innocence in me
Make a million without no sinnin' there'z no sense in It
And so am sendin' this, picture how my destiny iz
Restin' in peace, (preacher preach) & tell the kidz how It iz
Rappin', my talent, a form of promoting
You, better stay silent, It's evident, that you're blinded
And in my mind, am tha last of my breed dying
Hopin' to rize, teary eyez, though still tryin'
Still smilin' & wildin', hidin' the pain inside me
Save the best for the last, coz soon ama blast rhymin'
Keep a caution, hold back the flow of emotion,
Once in motion, niggaz fall victim to the wrath of my portion
Coz It's wicked, I used to kick It with a can of cologne
Who woulda known, a little nigga'd, rip the crowd on his own
I use to chill at home, nites alone & lites on
Rhymez thrown, am the legend, the world'z eyez on
Rize on, beyond the skiez, ain't no limit to when I spit It
I give it my all, spittin' It raw, now do you feel me?
Activities of captivity, now shown when I hit It
Gaze upon the blaze of the fury raized, when you set me free

WERE IT NOT FOR THOUGHTS

Were It not for opinion,
You'd have never related to my thoughts.
Were It not for tearz,
You'd have never seen me cry over my dreamz
Were It not for my openness
Guess, you'd have not understood my opinion.
Were It not for experience,
You'd have not expected me 2 talk sense.
Were It not for life,
I would not be living out dreamz,
Were It not for You,
I would never know who waz me;
Were It not for thoughts.

UNTITLED

Since I derail, tha' detailz that storm a nigga'z brain
Thy label me Insane, so am enslaved with fakes,
Takes mine, maintain liez, my truth contained in rhymez
In time, open your inner eye, so wisdom shinez,
Liez captivate tha' media, they lace It with picturez
While tha' preacher refers to scripturez, just to get richer
All due respect, can't figure, so I beg to differ
Love my neighbor & my blood'z plotin' to get a nigga?
Triggerz pulled, are the Jews God'z people or christianz?
They fightin', while we strivin' from sinnin', what Is the meanin?
In the end, am in Africa, forgotten & buried
to live my children in the handz, of dreamz & worries
Question religion coz am buggin' about God'z vizion
Doin' time in my Aunt's house, form of a prizon
What's tha' reason of my constant dreamin'
My inner being, in need to elevate my team
Wisdom glisten in my eyez, listen deep to my rhyme
God bless tha' child, who pays me mind; he'll rize.

UNTITLED

Give a listen unto my message, find meaning to what I say
Exploit wisdom, you may passive from my opinon & wayz
Bare with me, pardon my actionz to fulfil my passionz
It's only livin', one chance krookin' tonite, my satisfactionz
Preach reasons, alter decisionz in turn change conclusionz
disollusion tha destiny, of how you judge tha rest of me
I never meant to hurt nobody with my status of dream
Controversy

THE BIRTH OF A CHILD

’84, Here I waz born, in the midst of a scream storm
Mama takin’ the pain, az I came into form
Daddy long gone, mama twenty bout to raize a son
Hardworking, my mother strugglin’, A grain from the dust,
Givin’ her all to raize me right, And through all the crazy nites
Hold me tight, And so I swore, she’ll be my lady 4 life
No one could separate us. The love is strong mama
Appreciate all that you did, Though your gone mama
Six months without a sight of ya’ face or even touch
You can’t be replaced, That’s why I miss you so much
All the lessons given & learned, my crew, Is all I earned
Though promises flame my heart with hope and so I soon burn.

(It is presumed that this was written in February 2002 while Edwin was living with his aunt in Nairobi, Kenya. Edwin’s mother had left Kenya in August 2001 for the United States to pursue further education. Edwin was left in Kenya as he was in his final year of High School. His mother wanted him to finish his final GCE at St. Mary’s School, Nairobi before joining her. On completion of his final exam in January 2002, he later joined his mother in March 2002. He passed on in April 3, 2002 in his mother’s apartment in Greensoboro, North Carolina. His mother was at school at the time and only returned home to find police and other people waiting to break the news. Although it was initially reported that he died due to choking on an orange, autopsy results indicated that he died a natural death of unknown causes).

DEAR HEART

Y'

Hear Your Heart

Blind dream
full of thoughts negotiatin' with my brain only
Caught up in my mind
And am [illegible]
Mind blowin' and not knowin'
If I'll make it home
Dreamin' become my own
Grown and still am full of hope
Hard to cope with life
And so I breathe deeper
Broke and blind
Hard to figure
If I am gonna have a bright future
Helpless dreamer
Lost inside the greed to get richer
Inhalin' the smoke of livin'
Exhalin' through rhyme spittin'
Expressions of all my feelin's
Through words from all the talent I'm given
Pay close attention
You'll probably learn important lessons
My confessions
I'll probably die from material sins
Hear your heart

Hear your heart speak, hear your heart weep
Fear my flesh weak, fear I'll be laid to sleep
Hear your heart, stay alert, stay alert
Though we may part, I'll be speakin' through your heart

HEAR YOUR HEART

Blood stream
Full of thoughts negotiatin' with my brain cellz
Caught up in the mind
And am
Mind blowin' and not knowin'
If I'll make It home
Dreamin' became my own
Grown and still am full of hope
Hard to cope with life
And so I breathe deeper
Broke and blind
Hard to figure
If am gonna have a bright future
Helpless dreamer
Lost inside the greed to get richer
Inhalin' the smoke of livin'
Exhalin' through rhyme spittin'
Expressions of all my feelings
Through words from all the talent am givin'
Pay close attention
You'll probably die from material eyez
Hear your heart

Hear your heart speak, Hear your heart weep
Fear my flesh weak, Fear I'll be laid to sleep
Hear your heart, stay alert, stay alert
Though we may part, I'll be speakin' through your heart

DEAR HEART

Hold on, Don’t give up on me now,
Hold on, we have braved too many, for this one to cause us to die out.
Hold on my poor heart, you’ve got to keep pumping blood,
Just keep holding on, now It’s not the time to stop.
But a time shall dawn, when we can bare no more
A night shall come, and overshadow my bright star.
Hold on, just hold on, let me take my last breathe,
Before my death.
Let me embrace my loved once, let me see Shali
Let me cherish a dream turned to reality, before they burry me.
Hold on, Don’t give up on me now.
Let me brush away my tearz, let us go, knowing we held on.

THE HEART OF A LEGEND

There's some magic,
Inside the heart of a legend,
There's some deep passion,
Inside the heart of a legend.
There's the fear to lose,
Inside the heart of a legend,
Yet the courage to be the greatest,
Still lies inside the heart of a legend.
There's an undying desire to be free,
Inside the heart of a legend.
A deep hurting from rejection of the closest,
Inside the heart of a legend.
There's too much realness
Inside the heart of a legend
To be fake is an embarrassing stupidity
Inside the heart of a legend.
Creativity of great things Is found,
Inside the heart of a legend,
And from this comes a suicidal loneliness
Inside the heart of a legend.
An Idea is created,
And a feeling is achieved.
In turn an expression is formed,
With deep meaning and message to the wise.
Listen to silent whispers of the foolish,
And the shouts of creativity,
Cauze I tell you right now,
The wize do not see the heart of a legend,
Only a fool may understand and comprehend,
In appreciating the signs of a legend.
Check out your heat,
Do you see inside the heart of a legend?

LIFT ME UP

Lift me up

Lift me up, My Deserted Queen of nature.
Lift me up Because there's no more I can bare.
I have seen your oppression and I have seen your suffering
Our children have suffered, and have shed tears in vain
Lift me up, so I may bring back your deserved honour again
The scars from the heartless beating from other Nations,
Have disfigured your beautiful face.
But now I offer to take the place of rebuilding our race.
Lift me up, so our people may see me,
Lift me into the stardom of your love,
So that our people may also love me.
We have hurt each other and killed each other.
And In the depths of the heart of my forsaken land,
Lies the remains of my people; the heroes of this land
Lift me up, Dear Africa.
So I may uncover the dust from the sun,
And Its light may shine on us.
In God's hands, you are placed and in yours, is my body.
That I may be scarred, though I may die.
In God's hands I place my all so don't cry
With a gleam of hope shining in our eyes.
The faith in our hearts will be rewarded in the [illegible]
Believe in God only, I am only a man
Without a worry, Pride shall be reborn in this land.
Do not cry, For I have offered this duty, from heart!
I may die. But even though, Lift me up

Love [illegible]

LIFT ME UP

Lift me up, My Deserted Queen of nature,
Lift me up, Becauze there'z no more I can bare.
I have seen your oppression and I have seen your suffering.
Our children have suffered, and have shed tearz in vain.
Lift me up, so I may bring back your deserved honour again.
The scars from the heartless beatings from other nations,
Have disfigured your beautiful face.
But now I offer to take the place, of rebuilding our race.
Lift me up, so our people may see me,
Lift me into the stardom of your love,
So that our people, may also love me.
We have hurt each other and killed each other.
And In the depths of the heart of my forsaken land,
Lies the remains of my people; the heroes of this land.
Lift me up, Dear Africa,
So I may uncover the dust from the sun,
And Its light may shine on us.
In God'z hands, you are placed and in your's, is my body.
Though I may be scarred, Though I may die,
In God's hands I place my all so don't cry.
With a gleam of hope shining in our eyez,
The faith in our hearts will be rewarded in the sunrise.
Believe in God only, I am only a man
Without a worry, Pride shall be reborn in this land.
Do not cry, For I have offered this duty from heart.
I may die, But even though, Lift me up.

L_OVE_ E**K**uria

AFRICAN CHILD

The sun rises,
Another day begins.
Though it's brightness,
Blindens your chocolate brown eyes,
The dark continent,
Will always be your pride.

The gutter, iz your only way of life
No bread nor butter,
So violence iz your way to survive.

The other world,
Iz only just, but a dream.
Darkness fills your heart
And it's life to live,
Will always be a wish.

Cloze your eyez
And let God set free
The day, after the night.
Behold, it's light iz in you
And it will shine Bright.

Life isn't fare
But never despair.
God will alwayz be there
And speak to you in prayer.
Rejoice, for your light will shine.
In it is God,
So rejoice His name, Even in your demise.
I see your sad face, brightened by your smile
This is your day, little African child.

UNTITLED

Little dreamer,
I see ya', I hear your every prayer.
Your heart so cold,
Don't think that I don't care.
Little dreamer,
Just hold on, There'z much in store for you.
I know the pain you feel,
But soon this dream will turn real.
So keep you head up, Little dreamer,
While you stride through Africa,
Your bright eyez shown,
From the light of the sun.
I can see your hope,
I can feel your doubts,
But az long az you believe in God,
I know you'll throw It down.
Scared to die,
Makin' memoriez; Late night lifestylez.
I wish my hand could reach ya',
For now, prepare to rize,
Little dreamer

UNTITLED

So kid,
Don't think you're alone
When your daddy'z all gone
Cuz, I won't be Resting In Peace
Until I see you grown
Carry on
Nothing else could come above you,
You best believe I love you,
I never meant to bring you in this world of struggle
There'z only two places to go
Heaven or hell
Well, only God alone would know where I'll dwell
So stay tight
Keep your head right, It'll be alright
You could never be alone
When am dead and gone

IS THERE HOPE?

1'

No Hope For a Black Boy
So now what the back heck? I'll [illegible] got some talent
So now what the heck? There's no hope for a black boy
Even though I'm [illegible] to express the true passion of my gift
There's no one that will could change how I feel
There's definitely no hope for a black boy
[illegible] for I am
Take me from [illegible], to my hopeless state
It's a cold world my young world, don't take it easy
Cos even when I [illegible] this [illegible] eyes starved from [illegible]
I only realize there's no hope for a black boy
Stand up black boy work a miracle from your sins
Work a light from the blindness you've been raised in
Bring out the passion of a dream so unexpected
Bring out the expression of a talent neglected
I don't know what [illegible] me [illegible]
Perhaps the [illegible] I always searched for though death
But I guess it's [illegible] for me
There's no hope for a black boy right now
There's something about [illegible] in all black's
The hidden [illegible] and rage that comes out in forms of anger
The feeling of [illegible] enough, now it's time to [illegible]
I came up [illegible] when everyone [illegible] for [illegible]
Took advantage of young passionate dream of mine.
So [illegible] the world only [illegible] never [illegible] me.
It only took advantage of me so the world could hate me
[illegible] my [illegible] while it lasts
Cos baby, there's no hope for this black boy at [illegible] love
CHILLED [illegible], CAGED EXPRESSIONS
Rap is the way it's better I let you feel my [illegible]
[illegible] the world [illegible] attention
I guess you'll learn all this when you [illegible] It's no [illegible]
[illegible] with the burden of a unexpected talent
You'll be taken for granted! [illegible] there's no hope for this black boy

NO HOPE FOR A BLACK BOY

So now what the heck? Lil' boy got some talent.
So now what the heck? There'z no hope for a black boy.
Even though I try to express the true passion of my gift
There'z no one that could change how I feel;
There'z definitely no hope for a black boy.
Here I am
Take me home quick, In my hopeless state.
It's a cold world my young world, Don't take It eazy
Coz when I close this teary eyez starved from joy,
I only realize, There'z no hope for a black boy.
Stand up black boy, work a miracle from your sinz
Work a light, from the blindness, you've been raized in
Bring out the passion of a dream so unexpected
Bring out the expression of a talent neglected.
I don't know what awaits me at the end;
Perhaps the love I always searched for through my doubts
But I guess It's clear to me,
There'z no hope for a black boy right now
The hidden fury and rage that comez out in flames of anger;
The feeling of "I've had enough now It's time to rock."
I came up patient when everyone Including the closest
Took advantage of a young passionate dream of mine.
So damn the world coz patience never paid me.
It only took advantage of me so the world could hate me.
So let me spit my fury while It lasts
Coz truly, There'z no hope for this black boy at last.
JAILED MINDZ, CAGED EXPRESSIONZ
Ready to die coz It's better, If you feel my letter.
It's the only way the world'z gonna pay attention.
I guess you'll learn all this, when you finally know that It's no joy,
Being born with a burden of an unexpected talent.
You'll be taken for granted; Truly, there'z no hope for this black boy.

UNTITLED

I done been through all emotionz;
From shock, to keepin' a pocker face,
To straight breakin down & showin all emotionz.
I'm anxious to believe in real men don't cry,
If that's the truth, I'm realizing I am no man.

ALL WE WERE

A story of dust, dreamz & riches;
It's all we were.
An Ingineous architecture of heart, mind, skill in talent,
Waz all that we ever hoped to emulate from within us.
A multi-million picture within the frame of hopelessness,
Waz all we ever considered to be life.
A negatively Influenced race with the courage to rebel,
Waz all our closest saw us az.
Beyond the horizon of the mentality we were raized in,
Iz where we based our fruitful thoughts.
The difference in view & opinion,
Initiated innovative capabilities to rize behoynd our own limits.
It waz more of an emotional war than physical,
So we grew cold hearted.
A revolutionary voice of reazon in our minds contrary to other peoples understanding
Waz all we ever sounded.
A master plan & conclusion made of small pieces,
Waz all we were.
A forest in a desert,
A bright light of calm in a storm,
A dream that waz never meant to be,
THE GREATEST amongst the greatest;
It's all we ever were & all we'll ever be.

LOOK AT THE SKIEZ

So many tearz we've shed, so many close we had
Figure Iz a mistery, the misery of the gone dead
My pain cannot be felt, I pray cauze life iz hell
My jailed brain, so full of expression, only these rhymez can tell
Killed and so odd seemz, criminal convict,
They're obviously telling liez, Saying that It was suicide
Praying, hope for a change, while the bright, are laying dead
I wonder why must we cry, If our eyez are looking blinded
Strapped boots, soldiers salute, az we've always been used too
Only the wise, realize, how we've lost our roots
Something evil in my people chained in sin
We lost our wayz in this game watch for H.I.V.
Never lost my culture, All I feel is rap
Forgive my wordz az I burst, across this fallen land
And It hurts, to come to terms, of seeing us in the dirt
But let the sun shine, bring out a smile, look to the skiez.

UNTITLED

Sitting here with my peerz
What a wonderful dream
Screamz of wordz fill the air
Echoes faded of desperate hopes
Only wishing that you were there
In tearz and smilez
We shared the feeling of a sunrise
Living in Westi
Talking about when we would make It
Into broke handz we fell prey
Every single day
We sing just to pass the pain away
And in a dream
I waz afar reaching to the starz
And in the midst
I saw an angel bright smiling at me
With wordz of comfort
And I was no more at war
I felt a peace
Within the depths of my soul
Woke in the middle of the night
There I waz a shining star
Crying with my eyez closed
Not scare of the dark
An angel spoke
Dear God Here I am alone
As I drown in dreamy tokes
Help us rise from the dirt,
Of an African dream
Though my heart so weak
This is all my spirit seeks.

PLEASE WAKE ME UP WHEN I'M LOVED

Wake me when I'm loved,
For I can no longer bare hate,
Wake me when I'm loved,
Az I await my untimely fate.

Wake me when I am loved,
When you're ready to understand,
Wake me when I am loved,
When you're prepared to have me as your man.

Wake me when I am loved,
I cannot bare the pain of reality,
Wake me when I am loved,
For now, let me dream of this love.

L*OVE* E**K**uria

EMBRACE ME

Embrace me, cauze I need your warmth,
Embrace me, so I may feel comfort.
Embrace me, After looking at my teary eyez
Embrace me, For soon I will die.
Born alone, but never forsake me
Embrace my sorrow, stop leaving me lonely.
Embrace my wordz, Embrace my dreams
You've touched my heart, Dearly, Embrace me.

L*OVE* E**K**uria

THESE ARE TRYING TIMEZ

Am sorry,

yesterday took most of my courage & Energy,
so am weak & scared of facing today.

Forgive me,

I guess in my hope to share & chase my vizion,
No one noticed how much I tried, & risked my life for them.

I tried……..,

…..Damn!!! I feel so hopeless right now,
Coz no one knowz just how much passion iz caged within me.

Edwin,

I know the much I've lost, Iz special,
But the little I've gained, Iz true.

Be glad,

All you, who got to share in my dream and believed in me,
I am the dream, that wazn't meant to be.

GOD,

He brought me through all this, and allowed everything to take place,
He works in my dream alwayz, through me.

Am sorry though,

I can't give you much more of me anymore.
The dream Iz all I had, and you take It for granted.

Bear with me,

You've made It clear; I am nothing,
But what I did through those nights; those positive things
Are what make me unashamed of crying.
You rejected me, but I kept on smiling;
Clearly, those times, were trying timez.

I MISS YOU

I Miss You

And the tears kept streaming down my face
Flash backs in my mind
No one could take your place
It hurts, and so I cry
Then say you lived in a hurry
Too young to be buried
Emotions flowing free
And so many left worried
How could you die
Why did it have to be you
It is hard to say goodbye
Knowing we will never see you
Songs and poems of unconditional love
We wrote when we were young
Hoping someday we'd be stars
But now you're gone
We'll see you never no more
And all that we can do
It's just to cry and mourn
Will our prayers reach heaven
Will God take me too
Cause there will never be another one
Quite like you and I'll miss you

I MISS YOU

And the tearz kept streaming down my face
Flash backs in my mind
No one could take your place
It hurts, and so I cry
They say you lived in a hurry
Too young to be buried
Emotionz flowing free
And so many left worried
How could you die
Why did it have to be you
It's hard to say goodbye
Knowing we will never see you
Songz and poemz of unconditional love
We wrote when we were young
Hoping someday we'd be starz
But now you're gone
We'll see you never no more
And all that we can do
It's just to cry and mourn
Will our prayerz reach heaven
Will God take me too
Cause there will never be another one
Quite like you and I miss you

UNTITLED

Hoping to see your face
Az I knock on heaven's gates
I know your watching over me
From the sky's up above
Az I holler out your name
Come down and help me
Mama'z slowly breaking down
Missing her baby
She'z trying hard to survive
But slowly dying inside
Can't believe that your gone
And with us, you are no more
And though the time has come
For you to leave us alone
Hope to make it through
Az we mourn for you
Need you now more than ever
Homiez, I thought we'd be till forever
Tearz streaming down my face
As I wipe them away

MICHEAL DEAR

Each day ma' heart mourned since you walked out that door couldn' believe that you were gone, you were like ma' own, strolling in tha' dark, through hell you had ma' back wadin' through waterz of pain to fame n' be a star.

Like a brother I alwa'z wished for you kept it real alwa'z out for a mission n' never quit can anybody give me a reazon why you had to die, alwa'z by ma' side never once cauzed me to cry.

There ain't nobody in this world that could take ya' place, tha' luv tha'z in ma' heart for you it'll alwa'z stay thinkin' about you n' tearz fall, tha' memoriez n' dreamz can't believe that they be all gone.

Timez I wonder and aks ma'self why you really had to die. Goodbye ma' dear friend n' if I have to cry, keep me strong n' feel ma' song az I sing it on & on. Rest in Peace dear Michael.

CHORUS: N' Michael Dear, why did you have to make tear we shared so many yearz n' now You die here. Tearz rollin' down ma' eyez all timez you in ma' mind. I miss you n' each time wanna be with you.

Is kinda crazy how a day unfold, you awake in joy but end it all with sorrow. Ma' men George came over n' said Michael woz gone, I felt weak n I couldn' believe it could be him. Though I held ma' tearz back n' didn' react at that moment, tha' little pieces in ma' heart fell down n' were broken.

God gives life n' He also take it away n' if you make it to heaven, you'll shine on me like a candle. All that you left me with woz all sweet memoriez. Recallin' timez when you made me know life'z worth livin' for, for real. Tha' joy you brought forever gone be a treasure but why men why did there have to be an end you had it all rollin' now'z ma tearz doin' tha' sorrowin' once I saw that grave never before felt that pain

CHORUS:

Lonesome brother wanderin' with no destiny How could it be Mikee dying' in some disease. How many brotherz wondered why n' sistaz cried emotionz flowin' out n' pain mournin' for Mike. Somebody I sat with, broke into laugh with now gone n' washed away like a candle in tha' rainstorm. You alwa'z in ma' heart n' right there you'll never part. Men don't you understand what I feel for you? It ain't tha' same without you. Your family needz you. Piece of happinez that made 'em laugh brightened their days az you shone tha' sunz rayz. Now they left with rain clouds on da verge to brake down but got faith in God n' know once all this pain will go. You like ma' reazonz to smile n' now ma' reazon to cry why did you have to die but now I say goodbye.

CHORUS:

J
GAP

DEDICATIONS

TO YOU L.B

Sometimes I may refuse to hug you
Sometimes I may refuse to walk you down the road
Sometimes I may act as if I don't care about you/us
Sometimes I may refuse to kiss you
And that won't prove my love for you
Sometimes I may even refuse to say I love you
And that may put you down
You may loose hope and feel low
But what you should really know is,
We share a common bond
That every time I refuse to hug you
You'll get the best one out of me next tyme
The next tyme you & me walk down the road
We'll have the best tyme together
When I show you compassion you'll never want
to let me go
the day we shall share a kiss
You shall see it as a sweet dream where all
your worries & fears will go away.
It will be like a second heaven for you
When I refuse to say I love you, I know it won't
come straight from my heart, but
when these words fill my heart
show in my eyes
And my lips are ready to say them
They come from deep within & have a strong
meaning to both of us
the words sound so lovely like no other word you know of
the way I say them no one else can
yet my eyes can't show how much love is in my heart
And even though that makes you feel down and low
At the end of it all you'll be the HAPPIEST MAN
in the world
So please I urge you to bear with me
And share with me
this wonderful day that we shall all
TREASURE
HAPPY VALENTINE'S
MY LOVE
Always

UNTITLED (DEDICATED TO SHALI)

I’ve not been true,
But damn, I love you.
I don’t deserve your hand,
But you deserve to earn this man.

Can’t quite recall how we first met
Still I thank God for the approach proceeded from the first glance
No doubt you captured my heart’s essence
Guess It’s why am humbled at my Queens’s presence.

I wouldn’t bare the pain to see another man lovin’ my lady
But I’ve done you so wrong; Shali my baybe
Hard being without you’z being nothing but hell,
So this moment holding your hand; I believe am changed.
Hardly you were ever charmed by my thrillz az an artist,
All that thrilled your heart,

UNTITLED

Shortie in my life, come see tha' dime I plan to make my wife
Through tha' joy & tha' strife, I thank God, coz she be mine
Tonite, I gotta plan, to love ya', so let's kick It
Some sweet wine, she dressed up & damn, am diggin'
'member when we first met, memoriez unfaded
You waz sittin' at tha' steps in the West, gettin' braided
Overcome by game burstin', live cursin', I came to vibe
Damn your eyez, proceeded to analyze,
In my mind, was hopin cupid came in time
I truly love you, soon a nigga, finally made you mine

YOU DON'T HAVE TO

Let me hold you, cauze I don't wanna be alone,
But you don't have to hold me, cauze I've grown on my own.
Let the world crush my dreamz, At the palm of It's hand
But you don't have to worry, cauze Earth, Iz at God's handz.
Let me cry, cauze timez I get hurt Inside,
But you don't have to wipe my tearz, cauze It's not the first time.
Let the cruel breeze of shattered hopes, make my skin cold
But you don't have to give me warmth, cauze my heart iz cold
Let the scarz of my battles with sin, rearrange my beauty,
But you don't have to heal my wounds, for my soul perseveres.
Let me love you, cauze of who you are,
But you don't have to love me, cauze It's only my nature
Let me express, myself and heart to you,
But you don't have to feel me, just understand me
If this paper, could express my thoughts and feelings,
You would cry and share my pain and joy.
But you don't have to, for It would be a paper'z expression
And not mine
Let me appreciate you, cauze God created you
But you don't have to appreciate me, Am only a man.
Let the darkness, blinden my bright light
But you don't have to share your light, I've got a star
Let me live, knowing I could die,
But you don't have to suffer for my crimez just cherish me for the meanwhile
I love you, with all of my weak and lonely heart,
But If only you could love me, If only you could change my world,
If only you could make me happy, like I do sometimes,
Then I would stop crying.
Though I cherish you and though I'm hurting right now,
You don't have to feel pity for me, I waz born into all this drama
I just love you; I just love you so much,
But what you don't feel, You don't have to force It,
You don't have to.

STILL

There waz a moment in time
When I could tell how much you love me,
By tha' look in ya' eyez
And I could swear
That you & I were meant to last
guess now, am just holding on to tha' past
I met you yesterday,
And tried to act cool,
Didn't wanna, let you look at me az a fool
But damn It's killing me;
Tha feeling I feel,
Gotta let you know, how much I love you still

THOUGH WE DON'T TALK
STILL I WANNA HEAR YOU SAY YOU LOVE ME
DON'T KISS
STILL I WANT YOUR LIPS ON MINE
DON'T EVEN LAUGH TOGETHER NO MORE
ALL I WANNA KNOW DO YOU LOVE ME STILL
LATE AT NITE
STILL I MISS YOU SAYIN' GOODNITE
SEE U SMILE,
HELL I THINK ABOUT YOU ALL THA' TIME
I'M TRYIN' TO MAKE YOU MINE AGEN
ONE MO' DAY, KEEP IT REAL, SO YOU LUV ME STILL

"DO YOU KNOW ME, AND WHERE I'M GOING?"

A farmer plants one hundred crops of the same type and roots,
But plants one more, of the same type but different roots,
It's obvious that the last crop is totally different.
See my skin judge my nature, feel my pain, study my words,
Study my past, breathe psychology, worship your own brain and thank God,
But remember this; what is normal on this earth,
Is abnormal in heaven and vise versa.
What the spirit understand, only a man with the spirit
shall understand.
I refuse to accept the terms "what you see is what you get"
You may see me, but you don't see me.
A superstious heart, Iz either foolish or wise in heaven,
But an earthly heart, has no change for It is hopeless,
It is like an eagle that cannot fly i.e. useless.
A great man once said "I have a dream"
A prophet will not be accepted in his home town;
Too many people think they know and some have lost hope.
But even the brightest star has no light for day.
The rays of the sun are much brighter.
Earthly wisdom is foolishness and useless,
You can read all the books you want,
But not even the wisest of millions of words,
Could be compared with THE WORD.
To kill a lion, you must know how to cradle your fear;
You must learn the miracles of bravery and Its wonders;
This requires heavenly superstition and understanding of your own heart.

HOW GLAD YOU WILL BE

How glad you will be,
You listened to my heart & shared in my passion,
How glad you will be,
You tolerated my mistakes & you appreciated me.

How glad you will be,
You understood my heart when many rejected me,
When I waz cold coz of lost love,
When pain became a close friend.

How glad you will be
My emotional tongue swept you into my armz,
How glad you will be,
You accepted a rare true feeling of love from me.

How glad you will be,
Coz I have expressed much of my wisdom to you,
How glad you will be,
When you understand that I Interpreted my meanings clearly to you.

How glad you will be,
If the world ever mourns me,
How glad you will be,
When you realize that I was always in your heart.

I tell you now,
Listen to my heart beat,
And understand the meaning,
Of my earned wisdom,
Bump to the beat of my heart,
Az you listen closely to what I say.

Clearly you will hear the worldly material language,
But you, who's always been with me,
Will understand the soulful rhythm,
That Iz expressed In emotion.

Many have rejected me
But you've always been with me,
And when many shall ask of the dream that wasn't meant to be
You just don't know,
How glad you will be.

UNTITLED

And sometimes I wonder
Heavenly Father do you pay attention
At my lyrics from down & under bursting az expressions
The world, It took my talent for granted
Thought I was stranded, But you still made It happen
Now am laughin' at how you planned It
To my enemiez, who kept from seeing the light through my misery
I brought my dream to the mic
Clutchin' It tight, unto my grip, As am bumpin' this sound
Watch how I spit, fiery thoughts, At this stagnant crowd
Cause they could never feel me, am only out to make a livin'
Am hopin' the way you listen'z gonna let you share my feelinz
See really, my curiousity for wisdom & fame
Lost me in sinnin', Just to hear the world screamin' my name
Now, dear Mama, Dear God, embrace my passion to rhyme
Just watch It, how I turn despair, to a hope, so alive
And from the dust of An African dream. I know I'll make It
From the sole of a white man's shoe, soon as he shakes It
Coz it waz left behind, for us to make out a trace
So don't be blind, look all around, who could replace our race
I tell you, somewhere in my heart, there'z a hope for the people
So tired of wishin' make a million, from a so called "zero"
It took me time, to realize, the LORD was with me
Unto this rhyme, I dedicate, to even the coldest of G'z
Boldest they bleed, And no matter how hopeless we seem
Just keep your focus & dream, And don't be lost in the greed
Now It's upon you, to make out just what I mean
I came a long way. Just use my life as a testimony
Just Incase I die, cherish my breath through this land
My message I send, A dear letter to my friendz

I'M WRITING THIS TO AFRICA (My home)
MY PRIDE, THE LAND OF THE RISIN' SUN

WHEN YOUR HEART TURNS COLD

When your hert turns cold, It cauzes your soul to freez;
It spreads throughout your spirit, like a ruthless feeling disease.
The wallz that once were down now stand firm & tall,
Safe from hate, love, pain, joy, until you feel nothing at all.
When your heart turns cold, a baby's cry means nothing,
A dead corpse is trivial, mothers neglecting children is daily,
Loneliness becomes your routine friend, Deaths seems like tranquility
Sleep is unpleasant, If you even sleep at all, you forget Ideals
And turn off the reason, to make sure the product gets solved; you don't understand how I behave, wait til your
heart turns cold.

UNTITLED

We really miss you Eddie
We really miss you much
We really miss you Eddie
For the love that you brought in the world

Sorry I had to leave
But If It was up to me
I'd still be here
Making you smile through the painful tearz
Making you happy
Making It happen
LORD knows I had my fun
But now my work is done
I guess the memoriez are hard to kill
Wishing you'd cherish every moment
That you spent with me
Don't cry, Recall my words
Am always inside your heart
Am always with you.
Hoping you get this letter, Am writing from up in heaven
And Always Remember, Am buried inside the smiling caskets

Edwin's mom pictured with Edwin's school mates from St. Mary's School, Nairobi

"Edstudioz Edtertainment - Remember Me": Poems, Lyrics and Messages
by Penny N. Pettigrew on behalf of Edwin Henry Kuria
book review by Michelle Jacobs

"I will die before my time because I already feel the shadow 's depth."

Kenyan-bom Edwin Kuria had dreams of becoming a music producer and songwriter but tragically died before he could achieve success. Kuria left behind a trove of writings including lyrics and letters stored in his room—a place of inspiration which he called Edstudioz Edtertainment. This collection of writings curated by his grieving mother reveals an introspective, talented man on the cusp of fulfilling his destiny. Deeply religious and achingly ambitious, Kuria writes lyrics, poems, and prose glorifying and questioning God, celebrating his dreams of fame, and lamenting his fatherless childhood. Kuria also emulates Tupac Shakur and acknowledges his influence which is evident both in his premonitions of an early death and in his love for his mother. Through his writings, he explores themes of loss and struggle, hope and longing, love and family, and, ultimately, identity as an African man, lover of music, and fervent Christian.

The pages of this collection pulse with youthful energy and capture what it means to find your voice. Kuria buzzes with possibility as he riffs and rhymes through the hazards of adolescence and the heights of creativity. To read this collection is to witness a young soul awakening to his power and to his poetry. He gives voice to a generation of young people who see rap music and lyrics as an expression of personal experience akin to confessional poetry. Kuria also validates the global influence of rap music and confirms that rappers are poets. Both the foreword and introduction provide valuable biographical information that guide the reading and interpretation of the collection. Clearly, the publication of these writings serves as a living tribute from a mother to a son whose life was cut short.

www.ingramcontent.com/pod-product-compliance
Lightning Source LLC
Chambersburg PA
CBHW040527170726
48295CB00012B/370

* 9 7 8 1 9 5 8 5 1 8 0 3 8 *